Hiding in Caverns Formed from Old Roots

The Hsu-Tang Library of Classical Chinese Literature

Made possible by a generous gift from Hsin-Mei Agnes Hsu-Tang 徐心眉 and Oscar L. Tang 唐騮千, the Hsu-Tang Library presents authoritative, eminently readable translations of classical Chinese literature, ranging across three millennia and the entire Sinitic world.

Series Editors
Wiebke Denecke 魏樸和 *Founding Editor-in-Chief*
Lucas Klein 柯夏智 *Associate Editor*

Editorial Board
Cheng Yu-yu 鄭毓瑜
Wilt L. Idema 伊維德
Victor H. Mair 梅維恆
Michael Puett 普鳴
Xi Chuan 西川
Pauline Yu 余寶琳

Hiding in Caverns Formed from Old Roots
根老藏魚窟

The Collected Poems of Yu Xuanji 魚玄機

Translated by
Lucas Klein

OXFORD
UNIVERSITY PRESS

Oxford University Press is a department of the University of Oxford.
It furthers the University's objective of excellence in research, scholarship,
and education by publishing worldwide. Oxford is a registered trade mark of
Oxford University Press in the UK and in certain other countries.

Published in the United States of America by Oxford University Press
198 Madison Avenue, New York, NY 10016, United States of America.

© Oxford University Press 2024

All rights reserved. No part of this publication may be reproduced, stored in a retrieval system,
or transmitted, in any form or by any means, without the prior permission in writing of Oxford
University Press, or as expressly permitted by law, by license or under terms agreed with the
appropriate reprographics rights organization. Inquiries concerning reproduction outside the
scope of the above should be sent to the Rights Department, Oxford University Press, at the
address above.

You must not circulate this work in any other form and you must impose this same condition
on any acquirer.

Library of Congress Control Number is on file at the Library of Congress.

ISBN 978-0-19-777817-3

Printed by Sheridan Books, Inc., United States of America.

Contents

Acknowledgments xi
Introduction xii

POEMS 1

Written on the Willows on the River 3
賦得江邊柳

To the Neighbor Girl 5
贈鄰女

To Guoxiang 7
寄國香

To the Master Alchemist 9
寄題鍊師

To Secretary Liu 11
寄劉尚書

At the Temple of Washing Silk 13
浣紗廟

Selling Wilted Peonies 15
賣殘牡丹

In Exchange for the Mat from Scholar Li 17
酬李學士寄簟

A Love Letter for Li Yi 19
情書寄李子安

A Boudoir Complaint 21
閨怨

HIDING IN CAVERNS FORMED FROM OLD ROOTS

Spring Feelings, Sent to Li Yi 23
春情寄子安

Polo Poem 25
打毬作

Feelings at the End of Spring, Sent to a Friend 27
暮春有感寄友人

Winter Night, Sent to Wen Tingyun 29
冬夜寄溫飛卿

In Exchange for Li Ying's poem "Coming Back from Fishing
    One Summer Day" 31
酬李郢夏日釣魚回見示

Rhyming with My New Neighbor to the West,
    on Sharing Some Wine 33
次韻西鄰新居兼乞酒

Rhyming with a Friend 35
和友人次韻

Rhymes Mourning a New Graduate: Two Poems 37
和新及第悼亡詩二首

Traveling to the Daoist Temple of Reverent
    Authenticity, I See the Names of New Graduates Posted
    on the South Tower 39
遊崇真觀南樓睹新及第題名處

Sad Thoughts: Two Poems 41
愁思二首

River Ditty: Two Poems 43
江行二首

Hearing that Censor Li Was Back from Fishing
    I Sent This as a Gift 45
聞李端公垂釣回寄贈

CONTENTS   vii

At Providing Fortune Monastery, Established
    by Recluse Ren 47
    題任處士創資福寺

At the Pavilion Hidden in Fog 49
    題隱霧亭

Detained by Rain on Double Ninth Festival 51
    重陽阻雨

Early Autumn 53
    早秋

Sent to Someone as an Expression of How I Feel 55
    感懷寄人

A Date with a Friend Who Couldn't Make It,
    Being Detained by Rain 57
    期友人阻雨不至

Visiting Alchemist Zhao, Who Was Not There 59
    訪趙鍊師不遇

Speaking of Feelings 61
    導懷

Sent to Wen Tingyun 63
    寄飛卿

Stopping by Ezhou 65
    過鄂州

Summer Days, Mountain Living 67
    夏日山居

The Scene in Late Spring 69
    暮春即事

An Elegy on Behalf of Someone 71
    代人悼亡

viii HIDING IN CAVERNS FORMED FROM OLD ROOTS

Rhyming with Someone 73
和人

Across the Han River—for Li Yi 75
隔漢江寄子安

A Parable 77
寓言

Sad Longings at Jiangling—for Li Yi 79
江陵愁望寄子安

For Li Yi 81
寄子安

Seeing You Off: Two Poems 83
送別二首

A Welcome for Sir Li Jinren 85
迎李近仁員外

Zuo Mingchang Sends a Messenger en Route to
the Capital from Zezhou 87
左名場自澤州至京使人傳語

Following Someone Else's Rhyme Words 89
和人次韻

Guang, Wei, and Pou, Sisters Orphaned Young Who Are Growing into
Beauties, Wrote a Work of Such Peerless Quintessence that Even the
Snow Couplet by the Xie Family Could Add Nothing to It, So I Wrote
This Following Its Rhymes After It Was Shown to Me by a Visitor from
the Capital 91
光威裒姊妹三人少孤而始妍乃有是作精粹難儔雖謝家聯雪何以加之有客
自京師來者示予因次其韻

To Break Willow Branches 95
折楊柳

Fragments 97
逸詩斷句

CONTENTS ix

Appendix 1: Linked Lines 99
聯句
The Sisters Guang, Wei, and Pou (their surname lost) 光、威、哀，
姊妹三人，失其姓

Appendix 2: Yu Xuanji is executed for flogging Lüqiao to death, from The Little
Tablet from Three Waters 101
魚玄機笞斃綠翹致戮，選自《三水小牘》
Huangfu Mei 皇甫枚

Appendix 3: From Trivialities of North Dream 107
選自《北夢瑣言》
Sun Guangxian 孫光憲

Appendix 4: The Rhapsody of Yu Xuanji 109
魚玄機賦
Zhai Yongming 翟永明

Bibliography 122

Acknowledgments

Earlier versions of some of these translations have appeared in *Poetry*, *Ancient Exchanges*, *Voice & Verse Poetry Magazine*, and the fifth edition of *The Norton Anthology of World Literature*.

I would like to thank Zhai Yongming for permission to publish my translation of her poem in an appendix. Thanks most of all to my wife, Shenxin Li, as well as to Stephen Bokenkamp, Nan Z. Da, Wiebke Denecke, Grace Fong, Simona Gallo, Eleanor Goodman, Tammy Lai-Ming Ho, Justyna Jaguścik, Andrea Lingenfelter, Chris Song, Stefan Vranka, Nicholas Morrow Williams, and Muhua Yang, along with my anonymous reviewers for their insight, incisiveness, and support. All remaining errors, of course, are my own.

Introduction

Swedish painter Hilma af Klint (1862–1944) forces a reconsideration of received art history. Her work was not included in the 2012 Museum of Modern Art exhibit *Inventing Abstraction 1910–1925: How a Radical Idea Changed Modern Art*, but her first abstract canvases date to 1906, before the works of Frantisek Kupka, Vasily Kandinsky, Francis Picabia, and Piet Mondrian, who are usually credited with inventing abstraction in painting.[1] Af Klint's abstractions were not exhibited widely during her lifetime, and she willed her work to be kept secret after her death for at least twenty years, so the fact that she was ignored by art history is not a simple story of sexist exclusion: Kupka, Kandinsky, and the rest of the men who have been credited with "inventing" abstraction never saw her work, so she was not a secret influence on them; rather, she was a painter who did what they did, under the radar, a few years before they were doing it. The *Inventing Abstraction* catalogue explains that "abstraction was not the inspiration of a solitary genius but the product of network thinking—of ideas moving through a nexus of artists and intellectuals working in different mediums and in far-flung places,"[2] yet here is a painter who could indeed be claimed as a solitary genius, ignored because she was not part of the network. But just because her neglect is not a simple story of sexist exclusion does not mean that sexist exclusion does not play a large role in her neglect. Alongside and intertwined with feminist questions, then, art history must also look at questions of influence, of period style and the *Zeitgeist*, and whether something was "in the air," as they say, and at how history recognizes the contributions of previously overlooked or underappreciated artists.

Though the answers may be different, similar questions about period style and the exclusion or inclusion of women in literary history buzz around the work of Yu Xuanji 魚玄機 (c. 843–868), a commoner concubine and then Daoist priestess whose roughly fifty extant poems include some of the most arresting poetry in the already arresting late Tang style—poems that demand, I think, a new kind of translation into contemporary English.[3] By way of introducing her life and works, I will discuss what her poems

---

1 Cain 2017; see Voss 2022.

2 Lowry 2012, 7.

3 For another take on the relationship between abstract painting and classical Chinese literature, see Weinberger 2022. How many poems of Yu's remain depends on how you

INTRODUCTION   xiii

can tell us about a woman's voice and the thorny question of a tradition of premodern Chinese women's writing, alongside an investigation of the dialogue I see between her writing and the dominant poetic style of the day. These discussions will serve as my attempts to place Yu's poetry in the path of questions of *Zeitgeist* and influence, and the importance of recognizing previously underappreciated artists.

Today Yu is one of the most famous female poets in premodern Chinese literature. To reach such renown, however, her reputation had to overcome the patriarchal and elitist culture in which she lived and was evaluated, as well as the facts of her short—in fact, truncated—life. Most of the received facts—or "facts"—and opinions about her life and works come from two writers writing decades after she had died: a few sentences by Sun Guangxian 孫光憲 (d. 968) in his *Trivialities of North Dream* (*Beimeng suoyan* 北夢瑣言), and a longer entry by Huangfu Mei 皇甫枚 (fl. 873–910) in *The Little Tablet from Three Waters* (*Sanshui xiaodu* 三水小牘) (see appendices 2 and 3).[4] As one critic has put it, "Yu Xuanji's career is forever blighted by a particularly female type of embarrassment: a lovely prodigy with the disposition of a fishwife."[5]

Scholar Jinhua Jia has triangulated these tenth-century narratives against Yu's poems, as well as sources concerning the male literati with whom Yu associated, to come up with an authoritative biography.[6] Born a commoner in the Tang capital of Chang'an around 843, by fifteen she had become the concubine, or secondary wife, of a recent imperial examination graduate named Li Yi 李億, who was likely from an illustrious family. From 858 to 862 she lived in Hubei to be with Li Yi, where he would have held a local government position after having passed the principal scholar (*zhuangyuan* 狀元) examination, though they lived apart—presumably due to the jealousy of his primary wife. Yu and Li did live together in Shanxi from 863 until the third month (March or April) of 866, while Li served in the office of commissioner there, but he abandoned her when he returned to Chang'an in the fourth month. She became a Daoist priestess at the age of twenty-four, entering the All Suited Convent (*Xianyi guan* 咸宜觀), also in Chang'an. Given what Jia describes as "Daoist sexual practice, the cult of goddess, and the romantic atmosphere [that] legitimized the love and

---

count; this volume numbers forty-seven separate entries, but that includes fragments and some entries of two poems grouped under the same title.

4   The *meng* in *Beimeng suoyan* refers to the city of Jiangling 江陵 (in what is today Hubei) by its old name, but since the word also means "dream," the opportunity to translate the title this way is too good to pass up. Another translation of Huangfu's description is in Idema and Grant 2004, 190–193.

5   Da 2015, 682.

6   Jia 2018, 164–187.

sexual experiences of priestesses and helped to shape new gender relations," Daoist priestesses in the Tang took on active roles as poets and artists as well as religious practitioners, a liberty Yu seems to have taken advantage of, having love affairs with several literati—which Jia says "should be understood in this context of new gender relations, role performance, and motivated self-awareness."[7] The convent is also where she likely took the name Xuanji, meaning "abstruse mystery," as well as the parallel courtesy name or style (*zi* 字) of Yaowei 幼微, meaning "deep subtlety," rather than the name Huilan 蕙蘭 ("orchid"), with which she probably grew up (her rare surname, Yu, means "fish").[8] She was a priestess only for two years, however: in the first month (January or February) of 868, suspecting her maid Lüqiao 綠翹 of having stolen one of her lovers, she allegedly beat her to death. The killing was evidently accidental,[9] and while it is true that cases of elites killing maids and slaves could be tolerated under Tang law, Yu was not from the elite class, even as a priestess. She was beheaded that autumn. She would have been twenty-six.

After her death a rumor took hold that Yu had been a courtesan, or high-class prostitute, though Jia is at pains to explain that this and the corresponding label of "licentious" (*yindang* 淫蕩) are "biased and unsubstantiated."[10] The *Three Waters* describes Yu as having been a "daughter of a family from the streets" (*lijia nü* 里家女), or a girl from a commoner family. A nineteenth-century reprint mistakenly changed this to "a woman from a brothel" (*changjia nü* 倡家女), which has given some scholars the excuse to call Yu a courtesan. Additionally, some have mistaken the *li* in *lijia nü* to refer to North Ward (*Beili* 北里), another term for Chang'an's pleasure district, Pingkang Ward 平康里.[11] Her "ignoble death" aside, Jia affirms, "Tang people understood and accepted Yu's gendered identity as a Daoist priestess."[12] Her poetry was included in both extant anthologies from her era or slightly afterward, *More Mysteries* (*Youxuan ji* 又玄集) and *Tones of Genius* (*Caidiao ji* 才調集), where she was referred to as "Daoist Priestess Yu Xuanji" 女道士魚玄機.[13]

---

7   Jia 2018, 170.

8   Jia 2018, 166. Jia explains that while the character 幼 is usually read as *you*, her courtesy name should properly be read as *Yaowei*, with the character understood as from *yaomiao* 幼妙 or 幼渺 (2018, 259n19).

9   The *Three Waters* states that "[Xuan]ji was horrified" [玄]機恐. Jia 2018, 172.

10 Jia 2018, 186.

11 Jia 2018, 166–167. This would be like misunderstanding "a daughter of a family from the streets" as meaning "a streetwalker." The word these scholars are looking for is "lane" (*qu* 曲).

12 Jia 2018, 186.

13 Jia 2018, 186. See Fu Xuancong 1999, 682, 953–955.

INTRODUCTION   XV

Yu's story is fascinating, but her poetry is even more so. Despite her youth and her relatively slim output, at her best she is one of the most interesting poets in premodern Chinese literature, combining late Tang lushness with rare frankness in a woman poet's voice. Of course, writing in a woman's voice does not mean that she was outside or wholly independent of the male literati tradition—she knew the renowned poet Wen Tingyun 溫庭筠 (c. 801–c. 867), for instance, and wrote poems to him. En route to my discussion of what it means for Yu's poetry to be medieval Chinese women's poetry, I will discuss how Yu's poems relate to Wen's, along with men's poetry and the rest of the intricate and allusive late Tang style. First, I take up the question implied in my phrase "woman poet's voice," which is to say, looking into the notion of a tradition of women's poetry in Chinese and where Yu's writing would fit into such a concept and such a tradition. I will conclude with some remarks on the translation of Chinese poetry and the kind of translations I am trying to create in representing Yu's work in English.

Yu Xuanji's Voice and the Question of Women's Poetry

Chinese literature exists in, and as, a patriarchal system. In response, some scholars and writers have begun considering or constructing a women-centered lineage of Chinese poetry, which has at times centered on our poet, such as in "The Rhapsody of Yu Xuanji" 魚玄機賦 (see Appendix 4) by contemporary poet Zhai Yongming 翟永明 (b. 1955).[14] As Nan Z. Da explains, Zhai's poem "rebrands feminism as a layered consciousness of the sinological world, and a lyrical reclamation of its past literary cultures."[15] Here is an excerpt:

> she writes like a man
> socializes like a man
> takes the best bed, even when not sick
> doesn't bother with makeup under the tree a sudden fever
> a ruinous force   for now
> no one knows   in the middle of the night she gets up and combs her
>   hair
> reads through books of poetry
> she can see young men's smiles
> so why care about old men's bodies?
> why write poems of complaint?

---

14 Zhai Yongming 2013, 274.
15 Da 2015, 690–691.

xvi

Zhai's poem argues that Yu's "images, metrics, and turns of phrases were subtler and wilder, finer and bolder, than those of her much more famous male contemporaries," as Da puts it—though in invoking critics' reactions ("she writes like a man," "a ruinous force," etc.), it also emphasizes how "people have been attracted to Yu Xuanji for all the wrong reasons, playing up the received narrative of her decadent demise and eternal resentment."[16] What might some right reasons be, then? Would it be asking, with other scholars, if there is a female tradition in premodern Chinese literature?

The question has proven fraught. All but a men's-only club, Chinese poetry from before the twentieth century features only one truly canonical female poet, Li Qingzhao 李清照 (1084–1155), who has been described as one of a small number of "honorary men" in literary history, to the extent that it is estimated that she has been written about more in Chinese in the last seventy-five years than any other poet of her dynasty.[17] Even so, nearly everything ordinarily said about her is a patriarchal "refraction of what she originally wrote through the prism of elaborate interpretive schemes devised to make her acceptable to dominant cultural values,"[18] as Ron Egan has argued—which is to say, even for the "honorary man" of Chinese women's poetry, canonization has come at the cost of sexist practices of reading and understanding.

As for challenging the aforementioned dominant patriarchal values, many scholars have studied women's poetry in the seventeenth century, a time when women's writing grew in prominence, class and gender boundaries were crossed, and new feminine textual subjects took shape—but what about *before* early modernity?[19] In the second half of the nineteenth century, anywhere from two to ten percent of women in China knew how to read and write; how low must literacy rates have been in previous centuries?[20] Yet even among elite families, consider the way that influential Song neo-Confucian philosopher Cheng Yi 程頤 (1033–1107) described his

16 Da 2015, 683.
17 Robertson 1992, 64; see Egan 2013, 1–2.
18 Egan 2013, 2.
19 Robertson 1992, 99. For more on women's writing of the late imperial period, see Widmer 1989; Ebrey 1993; Ko 1994; Mann 1997; Fong 2008; Li 2013; Yang 2016; Yang 2017. For women's literature more broadly, see Chang, Saussy, and Kwong 1999, and Idema and Grant 2004.
20 Rawski 1979, 140. These numbers include anyone from "fully literate members of the elite" to "those knowing only a few hundred characters." As for literacy in the Tang, Charles Benn notes that it was "common for literate families to educate their daughters" (2004, 254), and Bret Hinsch writes, "Aristocratic women often found education extremely worthwhile" (2019, 92). Hinsch adds, "Book learning was not limited to the elite" of Tang women: "Even some prostitutes, courtesans, and slave women wrote poetry, proving that they could read and write difficult texts" (2019, 91). We do not have statistics for

INTRODUCTION   xvii

virtuous mother: "As she grew up, she loved literature but did not engage in flowery compositions. She considered it vastly wrong for present-day women to pass around literary compositions, notes, and letters" 既長，好文，而不為辭章，見世之婦女以文章筆札傳於人者，則深以為非。[21] In other words, the prevailing ethos toward the idea of women's writing for much of imperial Chinese history seems to have been: Don't! No wonder scholars such as Paul Kroll have stated categorically that "there was no discernible Chinese tradition of literature written either by or for women."[22]

Kroll made this statement in a (scathing) review of Jeanne Larsen's translation of poetry by Xue Tao 薛濤 (c. 770–832), one of the three Tang-dynasty women, along with Li Ye 李冶 (734–784) and Yu Xuanji, to have left enough work to earn them reputations as poets.[23] The three are often grouped together—indeed, the Chinese publication from which I take my source text for these translations, *Three Women Poets of the Tang* (*Tang nüshirenji sanzhong* 唐女詩人集三種), edited by Chen Wenhua 陳文華 in 1984, is one of many to combine the poetry of Yu, Xue, and Li in one volume.[24] They are individual poets, however, from different periods writing in different styles, so forcing them into one volume is, ultimately, rather strange, and only appears less so simply because of the rarity of Tang women with enough extant poems.

Do we need to understand women's writing as separate in order to appreciate it best? In North America the desire for a unified discourse of women's literature started taking visible shape by the 1970s. Adrienne Rich's famous statement that "women can no longer be primarily mothers and muses for men: we have our own work cut out for us" was published in 1972—the same year as Kenneth Rexroth and Ling Chung's anthology *The Orchid Boat: Women Poets of China*, in which American poetry readers were introduced to four poems by Yu Xuanji.[25] By the following decade more sinologists in the West were looking into women's writing in premodern China. I for one do not think it can be known whether Yu Xuanji had read the works of Xue Tao and Li Ye, nor do I think it matters. If we are asking, with John Timothy Wixted, "Is there a separate women's literary tradition

---

what percentage of families might have been literate, however. For a thorough treatment in Chinese of women's lives in the Tang, see Yao Ping 2004.

21 Cheng Yi 2014, 292.

22 Kroll 1988, 623.

23 See Larsen 1987. Both Xue and Li are said to have been courtesans, which explains some of Kroll's more stunning statements in the review, as well as Jia's need to dispel rumors that Yu Xuanji was a courtesan.

24 Consider Chow and Cleary 2003, and Nie and Levitt 2022 as well. A longer list of women poets of the Tang can be found in the table of contents of Larsen 2015.

25 Rich 1972, 25. See Rexroth and Chung 1972.

in China?"[26] or trying to rebuff Kroll's denial of a distinct female tradition, then our parameters are too narrow. Women wrote in the patriarchal system of Chinese literature, so they learned to write according to norms that were set by the patriarchy and evaluated by the patriarchy. The search for a *separate* tradition written by and only for women is what theorist Susan Friedman has critiqued as "gynocriticism," which Grace Fong glosses as a "women-centered and separatist approach based on sexual difference and the existence of patriarchy."[27] Even Adrienne Rich, often lambasted for being a separatist, does not fall for gynocriticism: the clauses before her statement about women having "our own work cut out for us" read, "We can go on trying to talk to each other, we can sometimes help each other, poetry and fiction can show us what the other is going through." Earlier, she writes against the idea that women have ever written only for women: "No male writer has written primarily or even largely for women, or with the sense of women's criticism as a consideration when he chooses his materials, his theme, his language. But . . . every woman writer has written for men."[28]

A better question about women's poetry, then, would focus on subjectivity and voice. I will assert that Yu's poetry is very engaged in the intricacies of her own subjectivity and being a subject. Six of her surviving poems mention fish, for instance. Fish appear often in pre-industrial Chinese, of course: when bronze-age Daoist philosopher Zhuangzi explained that "once you've gotten the meaning, you can forget the words" 言者所以在意，得意而忘言, he did so with an analogy with fish and traps: "the fish trap exists because of the fish; once you've gotten the fish, you can forget the trap" 筌者所以在魚，得魚而忘筌.[29] But the fact that Yu's uncommon surname means fish, as noted, makes their appearance in her poems conspicuous. In her poems fish play under lotus leaves, are caught, are eaten, and even hide, as in the first and most famous poem in the collection, "Written on the Willows on the River":

> The deserted banks are lined with emeralds whose
> mist is poised for entrance into distant towers.
> Reflections spread across the autumn water
> and flowers fall on fishermen's heads,
> while fish hide in caverns formed from old roots.

26 Wixted 1994, 145.
27 Fong 2022, 114; see Friedman 1996, 14. Fong's excellent history of feminism in premodern Chinese literary studies has been very helpful for me in crafting this introduction.
28 Rich 1972, 20.
29 Watson 2013, 233.

INTRODUCTION   xix

> Branches low for travelers to fasten their boats to,
> at night, the lashing of the wind and rain
> startles me from a dream, adding to my sorrow.

In a poem ostensibly about willows (but presenting a dreamscape where up and down are thrown into confusion), for their underwater roots to be concealing fish indicates to me that Yu may have also been hiding herself in the submerged depths of her poetry.

But how her subjectivity and voice link to the issue of women's poetry in particular is not a simple question. As Grace Fong asks, "how did or could women, the 'second sex' who occupied a subordinate position in patriarchal societies throughout history, articulate their subjectivities, speak their gendered selves in male-dominant cultural traditions?"[30] Paul Rouzer has even cautioned against demanding "a female voice" for Yu Xuanji—for whom, he says "class, social context, and literary conventions are arguably more significant than any effort . . . to write *as* women"—lest "we fall victim to a process whereby the differences between men and women are essentialized and rendered ahistorical."[31] And yet, sometimes the problematics of theory fall away in the face of poetry. Consider Yu's "For Li Yi":

> I left drunk. A thousand goblets couldn't rinse away my sorrow:
> departing tied my gut in a hundred knots that couldn't be undone.
> Orchids wither and will only return to gardens in spring,
> while willows tether travelers' boats both east and west:
> with or without you, I grieve for the instability of clouds
> despite how in love we must learn from the endless tide.
> When flowers are in season I know it's hard to meet,
> But don't expect me to sit here sloshed in my jade tower.

Presumably written after she had been abandoned by Li Yi, Yu here bares her heartbreak, even as she rejects passivity. It is very different from the typical poem from premodern China written in the voice of a woman (by a man, typically). Consider, by contrast, one of the Li Bai 李白 (744–762) poems with which Ezra Pound helped make Chinese poetry famous in English, "The Jewel Stairs' Grievance" 玉階怨: "The jewelled steps are already quite white with dew, / It is so late that the dew soaks my gauze stockings" 玉階生白露 夜久侵羅襪. As Pound explains in a note, "Jewel stairs, therefore a palace. Grievance, therefore there is something to complain of. Gauze stockings, therefore a court lady, not a servant who complains... The poem

30 Fong 2022, 119.
31 Rouzer 2001, 7.

is especially prized because she utters no direct reproach."[32] Pound did not say (he probably did not know) that the tradition has generally understood poems in the personae of abandoned women politically, as allegorical representations of the plaint of an out-of-favor poet to his political superior, in the implicit figure of the husband who could return him to good favor. This is not what Yu is doing here. Here, Yu utters a direct reproach.

Yu's gender and class mean that she can short-circuit the conventional metaphor linking the abandoned woman to the implied author. But Yu's directness should not be taken to indicate that her writing is unimaginative or artless, as women's literature—and, indeed, premodern Chinese poetry—have occasionally been framed.[33] Her metaphors bind the internal to the external. Knots, tethers, clouds, the tide: the world conspires to confirm her sadness. "Orchids" refers both to the flowers and to her name. Even when she is at her most straightforward and outspoken, her poems involve high artistry as well as strong women's subjectivity. Here is one of Yu's most explicitly gender-conscious poems:

> Peaks of clouds fill my eyes and let loose the clarity of spring:
> clearly, great calligraphy is born beneath these fingers.
> I hate how my clothes cover up these lines,
> but I raise my head, looking up at the names of these successful
>   candidates.

The title, "Traveling to the Daoist Temple of Reverent Authenticity, I See the Names of New Graduates Posted on the South Tower" makes plain the clarity that has been loosed: she is looking at the names of those who have qualified on the imperial examination, for whom she feels at once admiration and jealousy. As Wilt Idema and Beata Grant point out, this poem is "probably the only one from this period in which a woman so nakedly voices her dissatisfaction at the limitations imposed upon her by her gender."[34] Yet the title also indicates some of the art of Yu's poetry: en route to a Daoist temple glorifying the higher reality of a "reverent authenticity," she is brought down by the very this-worldly reality of her lowly position in the hierarchy of Tang society. The last line is particularly subtle: the name list must be hung higher than eye-level, forcing her to look up, indeed, to the names of the men very literally positioned above her.

---

32 Pound 2003, 252.
33 On the framing of certain modes of Chinese poetry as artless, see Klein 2019.
34 Idema and Grant 2004, 195.

INTRODUCTION   xxi

Looking up to men and learning from them even as her view from below constitutes a kind of critique of their power might be a good way to begin to understand Yu Xuanji's poetry. I explore this approach below.

Writing Back to Wen Tingyun and the Norms of Male Poetry

Today Wen Tingyun is among the three definitive late Tang poets, alongside Li Shangyin 李商隱 (c. 813–858) and Du Mu 杜牧 (803–852), and is known for allusive and intricate poetry. Whereas elite poetry in many eras of Chinese history had a tight relationship with the ideological buttresses of imperial and moral power, in the late Tang poetry developed, according to Stephen Owen, a reputation for being "a dangerous diversion from serious pursuits."[35] Wen was also one of the progenitors of the "song lyric" (ci 詞) genre of poetry, which was associated with femininity and which Owen has explained served as "the 'leftovers'" in the Song dynasty's "quest for ethical and political coherence"[36] in poetry and intellectual culture more broadly. Late Tang poetry has been called "decadent" (tuifei 頹廢), challenging and subverting the canonical modes of poetry; but the term could also be associated with the moral shortcomings of individual figures—such as "the poet/dandy Wen Tingyun, who," Fusheng Wu points out, wasted away "his financial resources and his official career while visiting brothels, then [got] into a brawl with the police and receive[d] a sound beating."[37] This moral judgmentalism could also feed back into the reading of poetry and find justification there: Rouzer describes Wen's as a "poetry of surface," as opposed to depth, a poetry of sensual pleasures including prosodic ones. In the eyes of more conservative readers, surface, "when written by men like Wen, is not just empty; it actually *conceals* the immoral mind that frames it."[38]

What would such a poet have to do with Yu Xuanji? Daoist nuns often exhibit strong personalities and intense feeling in their writings.[39] Part of the contexts of "new gender relations, role performance, and motivated self-awareness," in which Yu took part as a Daoist priestess, as mentioned above, included the writing of poetry. But Yu began exhibiting these traits even before entering a Daoist convent, and Wen had been one of her instructors in poetry; her oeuvre contains two surviving poems addressed

35 Owen 2006, 25.
36 Owen 2019, 2. On the *ci* in the late Tang, see Shields 2006 (especially chapters 4 and 5); on Wen's *ci* more specifically, see Chang 1980 (chapter 2) and Rouzer 1993 (chapters 2 and 3).
37 Wu 1998, 2.
38 Rouzer 1993, 10. For a defensive reading of Wen's life and his poetry in terms of that biography, see Mou 2004.
39 See Hinsch 2019, 80. This contrasts with Buddhist nuns in the Tang, whose "religion discouraged strong emotions of the type that writers expressed in verse."

to him. Legend has it that Wen met her while she was doing laundry and took responsibility for her education. Jinhua Jia notes that Wen had been friends with Yu's husband, Li Yi, and posits that Wen and Yu could have met when he was at the Directorate of Education in 866—the year he likely died, and the year she entered the Daoist convent after having been abandoned by Li Yi. While people have often speculated that Yu and Wen had an amorous relationship, Jia writes that there is no record of such an affair: Yu's poems to Wen imply only friendship, and besides, Wen was more than forty years older than Yu and famously ugly, whereas "she appears to have been attracted to young, handsome, and talented literary men."[40]

Yu's relationship with Wen provides one way of understanding how her poetry could have been part of the broader late Tang style, via its development through what *Inventing Abstraction* called the "network thinking" of "ideas moving through a nexus of artists." Friendship, tutelage and network thinking notwithstanding, however, we should not assume that Yu's poetics were a replication or extension of Wen's. The network exists because of internal tension as well.

In one of the poems she addressed to Wen, "Sent to Wen Tingyun," she wryly refers to him as the unconventional Daoist Xi Kang 嵇康 (sometimes Ji Kang, 223–262):

A cacophony of crickets on the steps,
clarity through the mist and dew on the branches in the courtyard.
In the moonlight they're playing music too loud next door, but
the mountains are visible above and beyond the tower.
On my cherished bamboo mat, brushed by the breeze
I send you the regrets my jasper zither creates.
You're too lazy to write me, Xi Kang.
What else will comfort my autumn dispositions?

In another poem "In Exchange for Li Ying's poem 'Coming Back from Fishing One Summer Day,'" she seems to allude to a line of Wen's about breaking a cassia branch. More revealing, though, are the poems where she seems to take what Wen may have taught her and reverse it.

Writing about a later era in Chinese history, Haihong Yang has pointed out that women poets "have to write in a poetic language in which they are often treated as objects without much agency."[41] Yang has looked at "women writers' appropriation of this poetic language" for their generations of "innovative self-reinscription and renovations in poetic forms and

40 Jia 2018, 171.
41 Yang 2017, xi.

INTRODUCTION   xxiii

aesthetics." "A dialogic approach to women's poetic creations," she continues, "means (re-)interpreting their dynamic interplay both with the literati tradition and with each other," to focus "on both connections, overlaps, shared elements, and differences between women's poetic works and the literati tradition."[42] This approach is also helpful in positioning Yu vis-à-vis Wen and the male tradition.

One of the hallmarks of late Tang poetry is its revival, with a twist, of some of the tropes of an earlier era of decadent poetry, that of the Six Dynasties (220–589). The Six Dynasties saw the development of the "palace style" poem (*gongti shi* 宮體詩), the likes of which were collected in the anthology *New Songs from the Jade Terrace* (*Yutai xinyong* 玉臺新詠) from the 530s. "A Random Excursion" 偶遊 is one of Wen's revisions of the format:

> The crooked lane overlooks the waterway, but
> all day its little gate stays shut.
> Red pearls on a mosquito net (cherries that are ripe)
> and golden tails on a folded screen—a peacock with nothing to do.
> This cloud coiffure could mystify butterflies in the grass.
> Her forehead is yellow. This limitless sunset mountain!
> "You and I are a couple like mandarin ducks:
> Don't expect anyone else in the world to bring you back and forth."

> 曲巷斜臨一水間
> 小門終日不開關
> 紅珠斗帳櫻桃熟
> 金尾屏風孔雀閒
> 雲鬟幾迷芳草蝶
> 額黃無限夕陽山
> 與君便是鴛鴦侶
> 休向人間覓往還

Palace poems are "primarily poems of a male social world," Paul Rouzer has emphasized, "written for aesthetic and erotic appreciation and meant to demonstrate mastery of language, of wealth and status, and of women."[43] He elaborates that the "quintessential rhetorical movement of these poems" is that of "penetration":

> The reader's eyes move through windows, behind screens, into bedrooms, through incense smoke, under coverlets chill from the

---

42 Yang 2017, xii.
43 Rouzer 1993, 77.

absence of sleeping bodies . . . Discovering what a woman thinks is the final act in a long, delicate process of unveiling, a final disclosure. For the male poets there is no qualitative difference between exposing a woman's bedroom, her body, and her mind. All are open to the manipulative control of poetic language.[44]

Wen's poem fits Rouzer's description nearly perfectly, with its sexual imagery (lane, waterway, shut gate, a phallic mountain in the evening that knows no limit) and its almost fantastical declaration of body-and-mind commitment.[45] The rhetoric of religious transcendence in the "back and forth" in and out of "the world" gives it a veneer of plausible deniability, but the thrust of the poem is unmistakable.

By contrast, some of Yu's poems move inside out, such as the poem "To Guoxiang"—or, better, "A Boudoir Complaint":

Selinea flowers overwhelm my hands. I cry at slanting sunrays
and at word that the neighbor's husband has come back.
The other day the southern swans went north, and
this morning northern wild geese flew south again.
Spring comes, autumn goes—it's missing you that stays.
Autumn goes and springtime comes. News of you is rare.
The latch is shut on crimson gates. No one's coming, anyway.
It isn't the thumping of laundry that transgresses my bed curtains.

Such poems reverse the perspective on penetration—though they are not poems about being penetrated (for that, see "Polo Poem"). They begin with the most intimate and move outward to the exterior world, where her addressee remains. At the end of "A Boudoir Complaint," the vaginal "crimson gates" are shut in disappointment—though there is still a sound, which I take to be sexual, making it to her bed and exacerbating her misery. Whereas the penetrative palace style poem asserts control of poetic language and of women, here we have Yu's poetic language demonstrating, without being any less controlled, the hardship of controlling her emotions. Her poetics are no less "surface" than Wen's, but the underlying motion of her poetry runs in the opposite direction.

So, does Yu write "like a man," as Zhai Yongming channels her critics as saying? On the contrary. The issue of control, in fact, returns us to the

---

44 Rouzer 1993, 74.

45 There are other readings of the closing couplet, of course. Mou (2004, 9) takes it as Wen speaking, with the poem about "the singer–prostitute whom Wen fell in love with and married."

INTRODUCTION   XXV

question of a female tradition in Chinese literature—or rather, it shows us how gender acts as a proxy for control. "Insofar as the female subject is concerned," Lydia Liu says, "writing is always a matter of rewriting (the male text) and gaining authorial control."[46] By now, in the time of Zhai, Yu's works have become an important part of a women's tradition in Chinese poetry created ex post facto. Yet over a millennium earlier, she was already rewriting male perspectives in the form of dialogue with them, working simultaneously with and against the patriarchal norms that governed poetry.

Of course, in dialogue, no one ends up with full control. That is the mechanism of its decentering. Such awareness may help understand Yu in translation.

The Edition and Translations

As mentioned, the edition I have used as the source text for my poems is *Three Women Poets of the Tang*, edited by Chen Wenhua. Much of my annotation is derived from this edition as well; other notes were suggested by my anonymous reviewers.

What does a new translation of Yu Xuanji bring? Her poetry has been translated a number of times into English, in part or in full, breaking down into a predictable taxonomy: poetic versions by writers of limited knowledge of medieval Chinese, and scholarly versions by academics demonstrating little attentiveness to contemporary English poetics.[47] This division has been in place since before 1921, when Amy Lowell wrote that a "Sinologue has no time to learn how to write poetry; a poet has no time to learn how to read Chinese."[48] Scholarly translators prize philological accuracy and sometimes seem to take a perverse pride in not letting their writing be informed by conventions of current Anglophone poetry. Meanwhile, on the creative writing side of the aisle, after an incredibly generative period in which the translation of classical Chinese poetry helped revolutionize the norms of English-language (especially American) poetry, so-called experimental translators are not very experimental anymore.[49] They have been making the same poetic moves—gerunds or infinitives to hint at the

---

46 Liu 1993, 43.

47 Extensive translations of Yu's poetry that I have found are: Wimsatt 1936; Walls 1972; Young and Lin 1998; Carpenter 1999; Chow and Cleary 2003; Kelen, Tam, and Song 2010; Farman 2013; Harris 2015; Larsen 2015; Ng 2016; Nie and Levitt 2022. Other translations can be found in scholarship, such as Cahill 2002; Jia 2018; and Jinling 2018.

48 Lowell 1921, v. As Wiebke Denecke and I pointed out (Denecke and Klein 2023, 215), James J. Y. Liu and Paul Kroll have perpetuated this division between "poet–translators" and "critic–translators" (Liu 1982, 37), or "between the sinologist and the professedly professional translator" (Kroll 2018, 561).

49 See Klein 2016; 2018.

uninflected nature of Chinese, line breaks taken from projective verse—for almost a century now. Such a division not only creates an artificial distinction between ways of reading poetry, it has left Chinese poetry translation into English stuck not in a rut, but in two ruts.

So I believe it is time for a new experiment, a new attempt to bring philological rigor and innovative creative writing into dialogue together. The translations in this book demonstrate my efforts at this: I believe that scholarly and literary audiences do not have to be at odds; both are looking for precision in image and of phrasing. I aim to be detailed and exacting in my treatment of Yu's diction, while also writing in English with attention not to composition by field but rather to conveying the rich denseness I find definitive of Yu Xuanji's voice.[50] Readers coming for the poetry must be able to trust that the translator is not passing off ignorance as inventiveness; readers coming for an interpretation of the Chinese need to understand how fresh Yu Xuanji can sound. In poetry, we cannot forget the fish trap of language just because we think we have caught the fish of meaning. In translation, we must rebuild the trap so that it can catch fish of the same kind. My target readership, then, is both scholars who can appreciate the particular readings I am giving to Yu's poetics, as well as a more general audience of readers of English-language poetry, who are interested not only in innovative expression, but also new voices from the Chinese literary tradition and new approaches to presenting those voices.

This has often meant making moves that others might not make. In "Written on the Willows on the River" (quoted above), for instance, I translate the first two lines as:

> The deserted banks are lined with emeralds whose
> mist is poised for entrance into distant towers.

Because the poem is on the assigned topic of willows by the river, willows are understood as the proper subject of practically every line—so another scholarly translation might judge mine as abstract, in contrast with the clarity of the poem within its generic conventions (not "emeralds," but "the emerald color of the willows"; not "mist," but willow catkins, conventionally compared to mist because of their cottony whiteness). Nevertheless, I think we can both trust contemporary readers of poetry in English to fill in these gaps nearly as well as premodern readers of Chinese could, and also introduce some of the conventions of classical Chinese into contemporary English-language poetry, even if we buck other conventions at the same time.

50 For "composition by field" and "projective verse" (above), see Olson 1967.

INTRODUCTION   xxvii

Two conventions that can be rethought, if not bucked, have to do with, first, the presentation of Chinese poetics as paratactic, and, second, enjambment and the nature of the line. The first issue, where lines, images, or even characters are presented as independent and not structurally subordinated to each other, has a strong avant-gardist pedigree behind it in English literary translation: Ezra Pound and Wai-lim Yip presented Chinese characters as juxtaposed nodes or poles between which an electromagnetic poetic charge might flow, giving the poem an enviable dynamic energy.[51] Over time and with overuse, however, I find that the voltage of such presentations in poetry has weakened. This accounts for my end-of-line "whose" above (relative pronouns as such do not quite exist in Chinese), making the second image subservient to the first. Mixing paratactic and hypotactic syntax together should, by now, provide a better sense of the dynamism of classical Chinese poetry in English translation.

The related issue of enjambment has divided literary and scholarly translators: most scholarly translators treat the Chinese poetic line as almost sacrosanct, translating nearly exclusively with end-stopped lines in English (though they often use hemistiches for heptasyllabic lines), whereas literary translators are generally freer with adding enjambment (Kenneth Rexroth and David Hinton come to mind) or, as mentioned before, spacing (Gary Snyder, Wong May).[52] About the above couplet, even scholars skeptical of Chinese poetry's ability to convey an electromagnetic charge between images would likely render the lines as end-stopped. But the complexity of the compound image—willow leaves as green as emeralds, against which catkins float like mist, ready to move into tall structures in the distance when the wind blows—recommends, I think, enjambment. That said, I do tend to respect the line as the primary unit of poetic thought, though I will occasionally add a conjunction at the end of a line to create a different kind of enjambment, and I am also likely to try to show tension by exploiting differences between lineation and sentence length, which I often make longer than a couplet or shorter than a line.

One reason scholarly translators may want to preserve the relationship between clause and line (or sentence and couplet) in their translations has to do with semantic parallelism in regulated verse (*lüshi* 律詩), a common form in poetry of the late Tang, where each character in a line will correspond to the character in the same position in its paired line in a couplet

---

51 See Fenollosa and Pound 2008 and Yip 1997.

52 In premodern poetics there is also the device of "paired phrases" (*huwen* 互文), where two lines of a parallel couplet are interwoven, comparable to enjambment but not identical to it.

(certain literary translators have played with this feature, as well). In Chinese, that is, the couplet

聚散已悲雲不定
恩情須學水長流

breaks down—to snap the words to a grid, as has become perhaps all too familiar in introductions of classical Chinese poetry[53]—as:

| gathering | parting | already | sorrowful | cloud/s | not | stable |
| kindness | emotion | must | study | water | long/often | flow |

The words "already" (*yi* 已), "must" (*xu* 須), "not" (*bu* 不), and "long"/ "often" (*chang* 長) are also "empty words" (*xuci* 虛詞), which is why they fit in terms of semantics or parts of speech. Once upon a time, I might have translated this as:

> Together or apart both are sad clouds are never fixed
> Kindness and sentiment must always follow the water in its
> endless flow

Now, I make it, "with or without you, I grieve for the instability of clouds / despite how in love we must learn from the endless tide," as it is above in "For Li Yi." This is another example of the kind of dynamism a hierarchical hypotaxis can yield. As for the parallelism, my feeling is that attentive readers will sense the patterning of the arrangement, without needing to be instructed to do so by repetitive lineation in a book of poems. And for readers new to parallelism in classical Chinese prosody, I invite them to go through the English to see if they find lingering evidence of the parallelism in Yu's Chinese.

These versions are my "strong interpretations" of Yu Xuanji's poetry, but as I have argued elsewhere, there is no alternative to strong interpretation when recasting the poetics of classical Chinese into English.[54] Every translation of classical Chinese poetry into English, even the most academic, is a strong interpretation. In this case, the strong interpretation I have pursued is to incorporate a scholarly reading of her poems into a dialogic

---

53 For a further discussion of this point, see Saussy (2001, 75–90), on how Chinese "lost its grammar."

54 See Klein 2018.

INTRODUCTION

engagement with a literary treatment that aims to highlight the poetics of her work, resulting, I hope, in a new kind of translation. And in the dialogic engagement between these two approaches to poetry translation, my aim is to find a reiteration of the dialogic engagement between Yu Xuanji's poetry and the patriarchal norms she wrote with and against, in the same instance.

POEMS

賦得江邊柳

翠色連荒岸
烟姿入遠樓
影鋪秋水面
花落釣人頭
根老藏魚窟
枝低繫客舟
蕭蕭風雨夜
驚夢復添愁

Written on the Willows on the River[1]

The deserted banks are lined with emeralds whose
mist is poised for entrance into distant towers.
Reflections spread across the autumn water
and flowers fall on fishermen's heads,
while fish hide in caverns formed from old roots.
Branches low for travelers to fasten their boats to,
at night, the lashing of the wind and rain
startles me from a dream, adding to my sorrow.

---

1 The *fu'de* 賦得 in the title means "On the Assigned Topic"; poems written for the imperial exam were on assigned topics and so come with this phrase in the title—but of course Yu could not take imperial exam (see "Traveling to the Daoist Temple of Reverent Authenticity"). Poems composed at social gatherings could also have been assigned. In some sources this poem is titled "The Trees Overlooking the River" 臨江樹.

贈鄰女

羞日遮羅袖
愁春懶起妝
易求無價寶
難得有心郎
枕上潛垂淚
花間暗斷腸
自能窺宋玉
何必恨王昌

To the Neighbor Girl[1]

Ashamed in the sun, you block it with your sleeve.
All spring you've been too lazy for makeup.
Acquiring priceless treasures is easy:
what's hard is finding a man with a heart.
Go, obscure the tears that drip on your pillow
and hide your heartache behind the flowers.
If you can still spot Song Yu
why do you worry about your Wang Chang?[2]

1 This poem is generally taken to be about Yu's own predicament, presented as if written to admonish someone else. Once a concubine to Li Yi, Yu was sent away because she did not meet the approval of his wife, and instead became a Daoist nun. For Jinhua Jia, though, the poem has Daoist overtones: Yu reminds her neighbor "of her freedom of choice as a Daoist priestess and 'semi-goddess,' and advises her to toss off her sorrows by taking the initiative in choosing and pursuing the man she desires." An alternate title for the poem is "Sent to Ministry Councilor Li Yi" 寄李億員外.

2 Song Yu (fl. c. 3rd century BCE) was a poet of the Warring States period credited with having written several of the poems in the *Verses of Chu* (*Chuci* 楚辭); I take his name here to imply a man of talent, loyalty, and deep emotion. Wang Chang is a conventional appellation for a charming playboy.

寄國香

旦夕醉吟身
相思又此春
雨中寄書使
窗下斷腸人
山捲珠簾看
愁隨芳草新
別來清宴上
幾度落梁塵

To Guoxiang[1]

Dawn to dusk, drunk and moaning with my body,[2]
I think of you. It's spring again.
Someone's delivering letters in the rain
and under a window is a woman with heartache.
To see the mountain I roll up my beaded curtain
then I grieve with every whiff of grass.
Since that last banquet where we sang together,
how many times have you knocked dust off the rafters?[3]

1   The identity of Guoxiang is unclear; some hypothesize that it was the name of a courtesan
    or entertainer, a role similar to the *geisha* in Japan later on. See Bossler 2012 on late Tang
    female entertainers.
2   The "drunk and moaning" probably refers to reciting poetry.
3   As in, with her singing.

寄題鍊師

霞綵剪為衣
添香出繡幃
芙蓉花葉【】
山水帔【】稀
駐履聞鶯語
開籠放鶴飛
高堂春睡覺
暮雨正霏霏

To the Master Alchemist

Colors of the sunset tailored into robes
and a fragrance crossing the embroidered bed curtain.
While the buds and leaves of the lotus [ ],
the mountains and rivers are sparse on the [ ] cloak.[1]
You stopped to hear what the oriole said
then opened the cage to let the crane fly.
Roused from sleep in the High Hall, spring
rains came down in torrents that night.[2]

---

1 Two characters are missing from this couplet.
2 "High Hall" and spring sleep invoke the "Rhapsody on the Gaotang Shrine" 高唐賦 by
  Song Yu; see Knechtges 1996; Xiao Tong 1994, 875–882.

寄劉尚書

八座鎮雄軍
歌謠滿路新
汾川三月雨
晉水百花春
囹圄長空鎖
干戈久覆塵
儒僧觀子夜
羈客醉紅茵
筆硯行隨手
詩書坐遠身
小才多顧盼
得作食魚人

1 Both rivers are in central and southern Shanxi province.
2 "Midnight," or Ziye, was a singing girl of the Jin dynasty (265–420) whose sensual quatrains inspired a subgenre.
3 In his Japanese translation, Karashima Takeshi (1964) takes the subject of these lines to be Secretary Liu, not Yu.

To Secretary Liu

You led the great army
and the roads renewed with songs and ballads.
The third-month rains along Fen River
gave the Jin River a hundred-flower spring,[1]
now prison cells are locked up empty
and shields and spears sit gathering dust.
Confucians and monks listen to "Midnight Songs"[2]
while guests get drunk on red mats.
But my brush and inkstone follow my hand
as I sit surrounded by poems and books,[3]
looking after a minor talent
to turn him into an eater of fish.[4]

---

4   The eating of fish refers to a story in the *Strategies of the Warring States* (*Zhanguo ce* 戰國策): Feng Xuan 馮諼 offered himself as a retainer under the protection of Lord Mengchang 孟嘗君 (d. 279 BCE), telling him that he had no special talents; when Feng was served food with grass utensils, however, he played his sword like an instrument and sang, "Longsword, let us go home! They don't give us fish to eat!" As for the "minor talent," some read it to be Yu herself, but I follow Yang Liu (2011, 65–66) in taking the talent to be Li Yi; she would be the fish that he consumes.

浣紗廟

吳越相謀計策多
浣紗神女已相和
一雙笑靨才回面
十萬精兵盡倒戈
范蠡功成身隱遁
伍胥諫死國消磨
只今諸暨長江畔
空有青山號苧蘿

At the Temple of Washing Silk[1]

When Wu and Yue plotted against each other
the Goddess of Washing Silk offered peace:
a hundred thousand soldiers put down their spears
because Xi Shi's dimples turned their heads.
But Fan Li went off in seclusion after he
ground Wu Zixu's country away (Wu died advising),
leaving nothing but a riverbank temple
by a small green hill, simply called Zhuluo.

---

1   A temple in honor of Xi Shi 西施, one of the legendary Four Beauties of ancient China.
    She lived in the late Spring and Autumn period, in Zhuji (mentioned in line seven but
    elided in my translation), now a prefecture in Zhejiang but then the capital of the state
    of Yue. The story goes that she was presented to King Fuchai 夫差 of Wu in 490 BCE
    as part of a scheme by King Goujian 勾踐 of Yue to distract him from running Wu. The
    scheme worked: Fuchai even ordered his general Wu Zixu 伍子胥, who had warned
    against Xi Shi and predicted that Yue would conquer Wu, to commit suicide. By 473 BCE
    Wu was weak enough for Yue to conquer it, after which Fuchai killed himself in shame.
    After the fall of Wu, Xi Shi went to live with Fan Li, the minister who had found her in
    the first place, on a fishing boat in the mists of Lake Taihu, never to be seen again.

賣殘牡丹

臨風興歎落花頻
芳意潛消又一春
應為價高人不問
却緣香甚蝶難親
紅英只稱生宮裏
翠葉那堪染路塵
及至移根上林苑
王孫方恨買無因

Selling Wilted Peonies[1]

I sigh into the wind. My flowers are always falling,
their scent fading in silence. And that is spring.
Maybe they cost too much, so no one asks?
Even butterflies find their smell too strong and stay away.
Red petals should only grow inside the palace;
could their emerald leaves bear all the dust from the road?
Just wait until they're transplanted to the Imperial Garden—
Won't you regret not having bought them when you could!

---

[1] Jinhua Jia's reads the title as "Unsold Peonies," rather than the more common "selling withered peonies" (see Jia 2018, 182). In her reading, "Like the beautiful peonies, Yu is unappreciated and unsold. Yet, like those proud blossoms, she believes in her own worth: she is priceless and deserves to stay only in the noblest palace—the imperial palace or the heavenly palace (that is, the Daoist immortal world)" (183–84). Idema and Grant, however, understand the title as "Selling Wilted Peonies": "One may safely assume that . . . Yu Xuanji is recommending herself to an undecided patron and urging him to take action before she is snatched away into the Inner Palace as had [been] so many other literary women before her" (Idema and Grant 2004, 194).

酬李學士寄簟

珍簟新鋪翡翠樓
泓澄玉水記方流
唯應雲扇情相似
同向銀床恨早秋

In Exchange for the Mat from Scholar Li

A rare mat unrolled in an emerald tower,
deep and clear jade waters recalling right-angle flows.[1]
Its feeling answers this mica fan:
both face a silver bed, sad that autumn is early.[2]

1 Yu repeats a line from Yan Yanzhi 顏延之 (384–456): "jade waters are marked by flowing in right angles; / nephrite springs are known for their rounded bends" 玉水記方流 璿源載圓折. Bai Juyi 白居易 (772–846) also titles a poem "Jade Waters Are Marked by Flowing in Right Angles" 玉水記方流. The image here seems to follow from the right angles of the mat and a comparison of its being unrolled with the flow of a river.

2 Both mats and fans would only be used in summer.

情書寄李子安

飲冰食蘗志無功
晉水壺關在夢中
秦鏡欲分愁墮鵲
舜琴將弄怨飛鴻
井邊桐葉鳴秋雨
窗下銀燈暗曉風
書信茫茫何處問
持竿盡日碧江空

1 The poems in this volume refer to Li Yi by his style name Zi'an.
2 Bai Juyi also has a line about sucking ice and eating bark, which became a common descriptor for faithful widows.
3 Places in Shanxi.
4 The *Classic of Gods and Oddities* (*Shenyi jing* 神異經), attributed to Dongfang Shuo 東方朔 (206 BCE–8 CE), tells of a husband and wife who split a mirror as they part, each keeping half as a memento and symbol of fidelity; when the wife has an affair, her mirror

A Love Letter for Li Yi[1]

Sucking ice and eating bark, wishes unfulfilled,[2]
the Jin River and Hu Pass in my dreams,[3]
I want to crack this Qin mirror in half. Sorrow for falling magpies.[4]
I play Shun's zither and grieve at the flight of geese.[5]
By the well, paulownia leaves sound off in autumn rain.
Under the window a silver lantern, dark from the morning wind.
Letters sent out into the void. Where would I go to ask?
I hold a fishing rod till the end of day, but this whole green river is
    empty.[6]

    turns into a magpie and flies to the husband to alert him of the betrayal. For this reason
    mirrors were often decorated with magpies engraved on their backs.

5 Emperor Shun was a legendary ruler of ancient China, traditionally viewed as living be-
    tween 2294 and 2184 BCE. In "Eighteen Poems Presented to My Talented Brother on
    Entering the Army" 四言贈兄秀才入軍詩十八首, Xi Kang has a couplet about his "eyes
    sending off returning geese, / hands strumming five [zither] strings" 目送歸鴻 手揮五絃.

6 In medieval China there was a trope of fish bringing letters.

閨怨

蘼蕪盈手泣斜暉
聞道鄰家夫壻歸
別日南鴻纔北去
今朝北雁又南飛
春來秋去相思在
秋去春來信息稀
扃閉朱門人不到
砧聲何事透羅幃

A Boudoir Complaint

Selinea flowers overwhelm my hands.[1] I cry at slanting sunrays
and at word that the neighbor's husband has come back.
The other day the southern swans went north, and
this morning northern wild geese flew south again.
Spring comes, autumn goes—it's missing you that stays.
Autumn goes and springtime comes. News of you is rare.
The latch is shut on crimson gates. No one's coming, anyway.
It isn't the thumping of laundry[2] that transgresses my bed curtains.

---

1   A poem from the Han begins, "I go up the mountain to pick selinea / and come down
to meet my former husband" 上山採蘼蕪，下山逢故夫.

2   This is a trope of autumn, as winter clothes would be pounded clean in late fall.

春情寄子安

山路欹斜石磴危
不愁行苦苦相思
冰銷遠磵憐清韻
雪遠寒峰想玉姿
莫聽凡歌春病酒
休招閑客夜貪棋
如松匪石盟長在
比翼連襟會肯遲
雖恨獨行冬盡日
終期相見月圓時
別君何物堪持贈
淚落晴光一首詩

Spring Feelings, Sent to Li Yi

The mountain roads slant and slope and stone steps slip,
but it isn't the traveling that's hard—what's hard is how much
    I miss you.
Ice sluices through a distant gully. I love your clear rhyming.
The snow on the far-off cold peaks . . . I envision your jade-like poise.
(Just don't listen to mundane songs, and don't get sick when you
    drink in spring.
Stop inviting over bores greedy for *go* at night.)
Like pine, not stone:[1] my oath is forever, even if
our meetings keep getting delayed, like wings[2] or else lapels.
And though I hate to travel alone, especially on the last day of winter,
in the end, I hope to see you. The moon will be full.
And when I leave, what gifts can I give?
Falling tears in bright daylight. Along with this one poem.

---

1   A poem from the *Classic of Poetry* (*Shijing* 詩經) contains the line, "My heart is not stone, it cannot be turned" 我心匪石，不可轉也.2
2   The "wings" here refer to a bird with only one eye and one wing, meaning it could only fly when paired with another.

打毬作

堅圓淨滑一星流
月杖爭敲未擬休
無滯礙時從撥弄
有遮攔處任鈎留
不辭宛轉長隨手
却恐相將不到頭
畢竟入門應始了
願君爭取最前籌

Polo Poem

Hard and round and pure and smooth, a meteor
shot by crescent sticks in competition, restless,
never stagnant, no obstruction, flitted and flung forever,
and if it meets resistance, let it linger,
don't avoid the twists and turns—follow your hands!
Or are you afraid you can't finish?
You'll begin to understand, once you score.
I wish you best of luck in getting it in the goal.

暮春有感寄友人

鶯語驚殘夢
輕粧改淚容
竹陰初月薄
江靜晚烟濃
濕嘴銜泥燕
香鬚採蕊蜂
獨憐無限思
吟罷亞枝松

Feelings at the End of Spring, Sent to a Friend

What the orioles say startles and shatters my dream.
Light makeup to alter a teary face,
shadows of bamboo, a frail waxing crescent,
a quiet river thick in evening mist,
the wet mouth of a mud-carrying swallow,
pollen-picking bees with their fragrant palpi . . .
I'm the pitiable one, endlessly thinking of you.
I'll stop these songs that depress the branches of pines.

冬夜寄溫飛卿

苦思搜詩燈下吟
不眠長夜怕寒衾
滿庭木葉愁風起
透幌紗窗惜月沈
疎散未閑終遂願
盛衰空見本來心
幽棲莫定梧桐處
暮雀啾啾空遠林

---

1 The poet Wen Tingyun (style name Feiqing) was known for frequenting brothels after failing the imperial exam. Perhaps it was during such a visit that he met the young Yu Xuanji, working as a laundry maid. One story goes that he took responsibility for educating her and she fell in love with him, but he wished for better for her and introduced her to Li Yi.

Winter Night, Sent to Wen Tingyun[1]

Pains finding a poem to read you in the lamplight.[2]
I haven't slept all night long—I hate this cold quilt.
The courtyard is full of leaves blown off trees by a worried wind[3]
and a sinking sad moon pierces the bed curtain and window scrim.
Dispersed, we have no time to carry out our wishes,
but in every rise and fall we see the mind in its original state.
Without a hidden perch in the paulownias,[4]
the sparrows circle the grove, vacantly chirping all night.

---

2 The line invokes an important principle in the crafting of poetry in the late Tang, *kuyin* 苦吟, which Owen 2006 translates as "taking pains in composition."

3 This line echoes the "Nine Songs" ("Jiuge" 九歌) from the *Verses of Chu*, "a tender autumn breeze / raises ripples on Dongting Lake beneath the leaves on trees" 嫋嫋兮秋風，洞庭波兮木葉下.

4 The paulownia, or Chinese parasol tree (*wutong*), is often used to imply its homophone, *wu tong* 吾同, or "we together." Another association comes from *Zhuangzi*, which states that the *yuanchu*, a phoenix of the yellow variety, "will rest on nothing but the Wutong tree" 夫鵷鶵...非梧桐不止 (Watson 2013, 137; Guo and Wang 2012, 607).

酬李郢夏日釣魚回見示

住處雖同巷
經年不一過
清詞勸舊女
香桂折新柯
道性欺冰雪
禪心笑綺羅
跡登霄漢上
無路接烟波

---

1   Li Ying (styled Chuwang 楚望) was an Attendant Censor and minor poet from the Tang capital Chang'an who passed the imperial exam in 856. His poem mentioned in the title does not seem to have survived.

In Exchange for Li Ying's poem "Coming Back from Fishing One Summer Day"[1]

Though we used to live down the same lane
you haven't come by for years.
Your pure poetry urged this old girl on, but
then you broke off a new cassia branch.[2]
Well, the nature of the Way deceives all ice and snow
and the Zen mind laughs at fine silk.[3]
These footprints lead up to the river in the sky,
but no path[4] meets mist-covered waters.

2   This means to pass the imperial exam. The *History of the Jin* (*Jinshu* 晉書), the official record of the Jin dynasty, tells an anecdote of Xi Shen 郤詵 boasting to Emperor Wu in the East Hall that he had "tackled the exam questions expertly, the number one under heaven, like a branch of cassia or a piece of jade from Mount Kun" 臣舉賢良對策，為天下第一，猶桂林之一枝，崑山之片玉. After that, passing the imperial exam was referred to as "East Hall Cassia" 東堂桂. Wen Tingyun has a couplet that reads: "Just as I delight in a friend breaking a cassia branch before me, I pity a visitor still drifting along like tumbleweed" 猶喜故人先折桂，自憐羈客尚飄蓬. Ye Mengde 葉夢得 (1077–1148) also explains this in his *Conversations in Avoidance of Summer* (*Bishu luhua* 避暑錄話).

3   Point being, she has become a Daoist nun.

4   This sky could refer to the spiritual realm to which Yu has devoted herself, or to the court, to which Li Ying has ascended after passing the exam. Either way, their paths do not cross.

次韻西鄰新居兼乞酒

一首詩來百度吟
新情字字又聲金
西看已有登垣意
遠望能無化石心
河漢期賒空極目
瀟湘夢斷罷調琴
況逢寒節添鄉思
叔夜佳醪莫獨斟

1 Yu seems to be positioning herself vis-à-vis "The Rhapsody on Deng Tuzi's Lecherousness" 登徒子好色賦, attributed to Song Yu: "Of all the beauties in the world, none are
like those of Chu, and of all the beautiful women in Chu, none are like those of my village,
and of all the pretty girls in my village, none are like the daughter of my neighbor to the
east" 天下之佳人莫若楚國，楚國之麗者莫若臣里；臣里之美者，莫若臣東家之子.
2 The reference is to "Husband Lookout Rock" 望夫化石, where, the story goes, a faithful
woman was turned to stone waiting for her husband to return.

Rhyming with My New Neighbor to the West, on Sharing Some Wine

A poem comes—I read it a hundred times
and word on word its new feelings ring like gold.
To the west I see a thought already peeking over the wall,[1]
though when I look far off, will my heart not turn to stone?[2]
In the stars the lovers' meeting is delayed.[3] Nothing meets my eye,
so my dreams are broken between the Xiao and Xiang rivers. I put
    down my zither.
Every time the Cold Food holiday comes around, it deepens my
    longing for home;
Xi Kang never drank his fine wine alone.[4]

3   The reference is to the tale of the Cowherd 牛郎 and the Weaver Girl 織女, whose love
    was forbidden and who were banished to either side of the heavenly river (the Milky
    Way), the Weaver Girl as the star Vega and the Cowherd as the star Altair. Each year on
    the seventh day of the seventh lunar month a flock of magpies forms a bridge to allow
    them to see each other.

4   Xi Kang (styled Shuye) was a Daoist, musician, alchemist, and poet of the Three King-
    doms era. A zither player, he was one of the heavy-drinking Seven Sages of the Bamboo
    Grove; either his zither or that they drank together seems to be the point of the allusion.

和友人次韻

何事能銷旅館愁
紅箋開處見銀鈎
蓬山雨灑千峰小
嶰谷風吹萬葉秋
字字朝看輕碧玉
篇篇夜誦在衾裯
欲將香匣收藏却
且惜時吟在手頭

Rhyming with a Friend

What can diminish my roadhouse sadness?
Where the red envelope was torn I see a silver brushstroke.
Penglai mountain rainfall makes a thousand summits small[1]
but the wind in the Valley Xie turns ten thousand leaves to autumn.[2]
With each word, this morning, I look less at my green jasper.
I will recite your poems at night when wrapped in my blankets—
I should keep them in my incense box
but would rather hold them in my hands, to read again and again.

---

1   Penglai, located at the eastern end of the Bohai Sea by Korea Bay, is a mythological island where transcendents reside.
2   Xie is another paradise in Daoist mythology, but also a valley north of the Kunlun mountains, presumably named after its mythological namesake, which is located at the northern edge of the Tibetan Plateau south of the Tarim Basin. According to legend, when Ling Lun 伶倫 was ordered to create music by the Yellow Emperor, the originator of Chinese culture, he traveled to the Valley Xie in search of the phoenix and while there carved bamboo into pipes to make sounds in imitation of the birds' cries.

和新及第悼亡詩二首

仙籍人間不久留
片時已過十經秋
鴛鴦帳下香猶暖
鸚鵡籠中語未休
朝露綴花如臉恨
晚風欹柳似眉愁
彩雲一去無消息
潘岳多情欲白頭

一枝月桂和烟秀
萬樹江桃帶雨紅
且醉樽前休悵望
古來悲樂與今同

1 A curtain surrounding a marital bed embroidered with images of mandarin ducks. Because mandarin ducks travel in pairs and are believed to mate for life, they have been used as symbols for romance and marriage.
2 The ancients rode such clouds when they first became transcendents.

Rhymes Mourning a New Graduate: Two Poems

The transcendents don't stay in the human realm for long,
ten autumns passing in a mere moment.
Under a mandarin duck canopy[1] the incense stays warm
but speech is still ceaseless inside a parrot cage.
This morning dew beaded the flowers, like a face in anguish.
Tonight the wind will bend the willows like a worried brow.
No news since you took off on colored clouds.[2]
Pan Yue is so sad his hair is going white.[3]

A branch of moon cassia,[4] as graceful as the mist.
Ten thousand river peach trees, turning rainfall red.
Let's get drunk on these goblets! Stop staring off in pain.
The sadness and pleasure of the past were no different than today's.

3 Among the most famous poems by Pan Yue (247–300), a poet of the Western Jin known
   for his rhapsodies and good looks, are his three elegies for his wife. The story is that he
   was so overcome with grief that his hair turned white overnight. In an interesting gender
   reversal, Yu is here figuring herself as Pan Yue.
4 "Cassia" is a homophone for "honor" (*gui* 貴); those who passed the civil service exam
   were thus said to have "plucked cassia" (*zhegui* 折桂), or reached an honor. See also note
   2 in "In Exchange for Li Ying's poem 'Coming Back from Fishing One Summer Day'."

遊崇真觀南樓睹新及第題名處

雲峰滿目放春晴
歷歷銀鈎指下生
自恨羅衣掩詩句
舉頭空羨榜中名

Traveling to the Daoist Temple of Reverent Authenticity, I See the Names of New Graduates Posted on the South Tower

Peaks of clouds fill my eyes and let loose the clarity of spring:
clearly, great calligraphy is born beneath these fingers.
I hate how my clothes cover up these lines,[1]
but I raise my head, looking up at the names of these successful
  candidates.

---

1 The implication is that she hates being a woman, as her poetic talent cannot be rewarded
  with an official position.

愁思二首

落葉紛紛暮雨和
朱絲獨撫自清歌
放情休恨無心友
養性空拋苦海波
長者車音門外有
道家書卷枕前多
布衣終作雲霄客
綠水青山時一過

自嘆多情是足愁
況當風月滿庭秋
洞房偏與更聲近
夜夜燈前欲白頭

Sad Thoughts: Two Poems

The leaves are falling everywhere. The evening rain is gentle,
and I strum red strings and sing myself a song
to let go of sorrow. I have no soulmate
so nourish my empty nature—to toss into a suffering sea.[1]
Outside the gates is the noise of elders in carriages, but
I've stacked the writings of Daoists beside my pillow:
I wear plain clothes now, but I will travel in the clouds.[2]
One day, I will pass by green waters and blue mountains.

I sigh spontaneously. So many emotions, sufficient sadness
despite the wind and moon filling the courtyard with autumn.
This cave of a room[3] leans toward the sound of night watch.
Night on night, my hair grows whiter in the lamplight.

---

1   "Nourishing one's nature" is a method of self-cultivation in *Zhuangzi*; "sea of suffering"
    is a Buddhist term.
2   Wearing plain clothes made of linen indicated being a commoner, as opposed to an
    aristocrat, who would have worn silk.
3   The term refers to the bridal chamber.

江行二首

大江橫抱武昌斜
鸚鵡洲前萬戶家
畫舸春眠朝未足
夢為蝴蝶也尋花

烟花已入鸝鸘港
畫舸猶題鸚鵡洲
醉臥醒吟都不覺
今朝驚在漢江頭

River Ditty: Two Poems

The big river cradles Wuchang slantwise.
Ten thousand homes face Parrot Isle, yet
you're underslept each spring morning on a painted boat,
having dreamt you were a butterfly scouring for flowers.[1]

The puffs of mist have made their way to Cormorant Harbor
while the painted boat floats by Parrot Isle.
Passing out drunk, singing when sober, stuporous in both,
I was shocked this morning gaining consciousness at the mouth of the
    Han.

---

1   The reference is to Zhuangzi, who famously dreamt he was a butterfly and woke wondering if he was anything more than a butterfly's dream.

聞李端公垂釣回寄贈

無限荷香染暑衣
阮郎何處弄船歸
自慚不及鴛鴦侶
猶得雙雙近釣磯

Hearing that Censor Li Was Back from Fishing I Sent This as a Gift

Your summer clothes are stained with the endless scent of lotus—
where are you bringing your boat back from, Master Ruan?[1]
How sorry I am we never paired up like those mandarin ducks
who must have swum past your fishing rock two by two.

---

1   The allusion is to the semi-legendary Ruan Zhao 阮肇 of the Han dynasty, described in the *Stories of Darkness and Brightness* (*Youming lu* 幽明錄). He and Liu Chen 劉晨 went up Tiantai Mountain to pick medicinal herbs but met two maidens along the way; they spent what they experienced as a year and a half with them, only to find out upon their return to their village that hundreds of years had passed by. See Chan 2008.

題任處士創資福寺

幽人創奇境
遊客駐行程
粉壁空留字
蓮宮未有名
鑿池泉自出
開徑草重生
百尺金輪閣
當川豁眼明

---

1 The first word of the title indicates that this poem was written on the wall.
2 That is, a Buddhist palace, a temple.

At Providing Fortune Monastery, Established by Recluse Ren

A recluse creates such a fantastic realm
that visitors halt their journeys to see, so
on your whitewashed walls I've left my vain writings.[1]
At this lotus palace[2] with no name yet
where you drilled a pool and a spring erupted,[3]
you blazed a trail but the grass grew back.[4]
A golden wheel pavilion[5] one hundred feet high:
before the river, your eyes will be clear.

---

3 This alludes to an episode in the *Lotus Sutra*, in which the Buddha compares the seeking of the Dharma to a man drilling a well. See Hurvitz 2009, 163–164. Of course, Yu may have been describing the drilling of a literal well, but her phrasing resonates with a Buddhist text, to fit the description of a Buddhist monastery.

4 This might refer to the "plant that is reborn" (*chongsheng hua* 重生華), with which commentators gloss the *pāṭala* 波羅羅 mentioned in chapter 19 of the *Lotus Sutra*.

5 Again, meaning the temple in question. "Golden wheel" is the first of the seven treasures of the wheel-turning sage kings.

題隱霧亭

春花秋月入詩篇
白日清宵是散仙
空捲珠簾不曾下
長移一榻對山眠

At the Pavilion Hidden in Fog

Spring flowers and autumn moons put in poems,
an idle immortal[1] day and night:
I rolled up my beaded curtain once and never let it down
and keep my divan facing the mountains while I sleep.

---

1 A transcendent with no position in Daoism's celestial bureaucracy.

重陽阻雨

滿庭黃菊籬邊坼
兩朵芙蓉鏡裏開
落帽臺前風雨阻
不知何處醉金杯

---

1 The ninth day of the ninth lunar month. Because nine is associated with *yang*, or masculine and bright qualities, this day is supposed to be auspicious. Even today Chinese families celebrate the day by paying their respects at the graves of their ancestors, feasting, and appreciating chrysanthemums.

2 The last word of the line in Chinese is *che* 坼, but it has often been misread or misprinted as *chai* 拆 or *zhe* 折.

Detained by Rain on Double Ninth Festival[1]

Chrysanthemums throughout the courtyard, sprouting[2] by the fence,
two hibiscuses blooming as in a mirror.
Detained by wind and rain at Dropped Hat Pagoda[3]
I don't know where to get drunk with golden cups.

3 A pagoda northwest of Jingzhou, in present-day Hubei. One year on Double Yang Day
at a banquet hosted by General Huan Wen 桓溫 (312–373) the wind blew off the hat of
statesman Meng Jia 孟嘉, who seemed not to notice; when Meng left to use the restroom,
someone wrote a verse mocking him. When Meng returned he tossed off a retort that
was so impressive that Double Yang Day became known as the Moment of the Fallen
Hat. Li Bai wrote a poem that alludes to the event, "Drinking at Dragon Mountain on
the Ninth" 九日龍山飲.

早秋

嫩菊含新彩
遠山閑夕烟
涼風驚綠樹
清韻入朱弦
思婦機中錦
征人塞外天
雁飛魚在水
書信若為傳

Early Autumn

Tender chrysanthemums hold new colors, and
in the distant mountains dusk mist idles.
A cool wind startles the green trees—
clear rhymes to meld with red strings.
A longing woman, brocade in her loom,
someone trekking through the sky beyond the pass:
wild geese fly, fish are in the water,[1]
and letters, too, get sent along.

---

1 The trope was that both geese and fish could carry letters.

感懷寄人

恨寄朱弦上
含情意不任
早知雲雨會
未起蕙蘭心
灼灼桃兼李
無妨國士尋
蒼蒼松與桂
仍羨世人欽
月色苔堦淨
歌聲竹院深
門前紅葉地
不掃待知音

Sent to Someone as an Expression of How I Feel

The regrets sent out on these red strings
harbor my feelings but don't divulge my thoughts:
if I had known of the encounter of cloud and rain[1]
would my orchid heart have risen up?
Conflagrations of peach and plum blossom
barely block the pursuits of a knight of the realm.
Blue-green pine and osmanthus:
yes I'm still jealous of worldly admiration.
The color of moonlight washes over mossy steps and
the sound of singing is deep in the bamboo courtyard,
I don't sweep the red leaf ground before the gate:
I wait for the one who will know my song.

---

[1] A reference to lines voiced by the maiden of Wu Mountain 巫山之女 in Song Yu's "Rhapsody on the Gaotang Shrine": "At dawn I am morning clouds, at evening driving rain" 旦為朝雲，暮為行雨. In the Tang, clouds and rain were a reference to an amorous but fleeting encounter with a goddess. For more, see Schafer 1973.

期友人阻雨不至

雁魚空有信
雞黍恨無期
閉戶方籠月
褰簾已散絲
近泉鳴砌畔
遠浪漲江湄
鄉思悲秋客
愁吟五字詩

A Date with a Friend Who Couldn't Make It, Being Detained by Rain

There is no point for geese and fish to carry letters:
I made chicken and millet, but we neglected to confirm our date.
A shut door encloses the moon, so I
lift the curtain. Strands of scattered silk[1]
allow nearby springs to sing past brick embankments
and waves from far away to crash on riverbanks.
Homesick traveler, sorrowful autumn guest,
I recite this sad eight-line poem of mine for you.

---

1 That is, rain, described here as silk threads not just for the imagery but for the pun on "longing" (*si* 思) for someone, pronounced the same as "silk."

訪趙鍊師不遇

何處同仙侶
青衣獨在家
暖爐留煮藥
鄰院為煎茶
畫壁燈光暗
幡竿日影斜
殷勤重回首
墙外數枝花

Visiting Alchemist Zhao,[1] Who Was Not There

Where is the alchemist, off with the transcendents?
Dark robes[2] alone at home with
the stove still warm from herbs left boiling,
tea roasting in the courtyard next door.
The painted walls are dark in the lamplight
and the shadow of the flagpole is slanting.
I turn my head, eagerly, and more than once,
but it's only flowers on the branches beyond the wall.

---

1 Idema and Grant (2004, 189) say Zhao was "most likely a nun."
2 A synecdoche for a Daoist apprentice, who would wear such clothes.

導懷

閑散身無事
風光獨自遊
斷雲江上月
解纜海中舟
琴弄蕭梁寺
詩吟庾亮樓
叢篁堪作伴
片石好為儔
燕雀徒為貴
金銀志不求
滿杯春酒綠
對月夜窗幽
遶砌澄清沼
抽簪映細流
臥床書冊遍
半醉起梳頭

---

1   The *Miscellany from the South Face of Mount Du* (*Duyang zabian* 杜陽雜編) by Su E 蘇
鶚 (dates unknown) of the late Tang explains that Emperor Wu of the Liang (personal
name Xiao Yan 蕭衍, r. 502–549) "loved the Buddha and had a temple built, for which
he ordered Xiao Ziyun [487–549] to calligraph the word Xiao in 'flying white' style,
thereby naming it Xiao Temple" 好佛造浮屠，命蕭子雲飛白大書曰蕭寺; afterward,
"Xiao Temple" often appeared in poems. Yu Liang Tower refers to Southern Tower 南樓
in Wuchang, built in the time of Yu Liang (289–340), military general of the Jin dynasty.

Speaking of Feelings

At leisure, nothing will worry me
wandering alone through the light and breeze,
moon rising over the river through a break in the clouds:
a boat unmoored on the sea.
I will strum my zither at Xiao Temple
and recite poems in Yu Liang Tower,[1]
my companions bamboo thickets and
a stele of flagstone my best peer.
Swallows and sparrows are all I value;[2]
no aspirations for silver or gold:
my cups are filled with the green of springtime wine.
My window is dark at night, against the moon.
A clear pool winding around steps,
I pull out my hairpin[3] in the mirror of the stream.
I was lying down, books everywhere,
but get up half drunk to brush my hair.

2   As it says in "The House of Chen She" 陳涉世家 in the *Records of the Historian* (*Shiji* 史
    記) (alluding to *Zhuangzi*), "How can swallows and sparrows know the ambition of the
    swan" 燕雀安知鴻鵠之志? Yu is saying here that she is lowly and unambitious (although,
    as in *Zhuangzi*, the lowly are wiser than the mighty, so long as they are cognizant of their
    own situation).
3   Rather than a gesture of letting down one's hair, removing the bureaucratic hairpin was
    a symbol of giving up office. Here, Yu uses an image of male reclusion to represent her
    own idleness.

寄飛卿

堦砌亂蛩鳴
庭柯烟露清
月中鄰樂響
樓上遠山明
珍簟涼風着
瑤琴寄恨生
嵇君懶書札
底物慰秋情

Sent to Wen Tingyun[1]

A cacophony of crickets on the steps,
clarity through the mist and dew on the branches in the courtyard.
In the moonlight they're playing music too loud next door, but
the mountains are visible above and beyond the tower.
On my cherished bamboo mat, brushed by the breeze
I send you the regrets my jasper zither creates.
You're too lazy to write me, Xi Kang.
What else will comfort my autumn dispositions?

---

1   See note 1 in "Winter Night, Sent to Wen Tingyun"

過鄂州

柳拂蘭橈花滿枝
石城城下暮帆遲
折碑峰上三閭墓
遠火山頭五馬旗
白雪調高題舊寺
陽春歌在換新詞
莫愁魂逐清江去
空使行人萬首詩

1 In Hubei, just east of Wuhan.
2 Also in Hubei.
3 Qu Yuan 屈原 (c. 340–278 BCE), statesman and first named poet in Chinese literary history, purported author of the *Verses of Chu*.

Stopping by Ezhou[1]

The willow brushes the boneset oars. Flowers cover the branches
and evening sails are slow beneath Stone City's city walls.[2]
The tomb of Qu Yuan[3] on Broken Stele peak
and another mountain with distant fires and a five-horse flag.[4]
White Snow is noble: I write it on the old temple wall
and make up words to what's left of Spring Sunshine.[5]
Worriless[6] souls flowing away with pure rivers—
only to give rise to ten thousand useless travelers' poems.

4   The flag is the sign of the local governor. *Yuanhuo shan* may also be a proper name—
    "Distant Fire Mountain."
5   *Yangchun baixue* 陽春白雪 was the name of a piece of ancient Chu music. Probably one
    song, it was later interpreted as two: "Spring Sunshine" and "White Snow."
6   "Worriless" was the name of a singing girl in Stone City.

夏日山居

移得仙居此地來
花叢自遍不曾栽
庭前亞樹張衣桁
坐上新泉泛酒杯
軒檻暗傳深竹徑
綺羅長擁亂書堆
閑乘畫舫吟明月
信任輕風吹却回

Summer Days, Mountain Living

I've moved to this place where transcendents reside
and flowers proliferate without having been planted.
In the front yard I hang my clothes out on small trees
and go sit by the new spring, winecups sent all over:[1]
corridor railings intimate a path through the deep bamboo;
fine silk now bunches around my heaps of books.
Whenever I want I ride in my painted boat. I recite poems to
    the moon
and trust the breeze to blow me back home.

---

1   This may be an allusion to the game "floating goblets" (流觴) immortalized by master
calligrapher Wang Xizhi 王羲之 (303–361) in his "Preface" to *Poems Composed at the
Orchid Pavilion* (*Lanting ji xu* 蘭亭集序): "and there was a clear stream with little rapids
that enhanced the area, and we played floating goblets at a bend, sitting in rows by the
water. There was no music, but as we drank and composed poetry, we chatted cheerfully
of the nuances of our sentiments."

暮春即事

深巷窮門少侶儔
阮郎唯有夢中留
香飄羅綺誰家席
風送歌聲何處樓
街近鼓鼙喧曉睡
庭閑鵲語亂春愁
安能追逐人間事
萬里身同不繫舟

The Scene in Late Spring

An impoverished home at the end of the lane. No companions, either,
except for a lover[1] who stays in my dreams.
Wafting fragrances, fine silk? A banquet in some other house,
some other tower the wind is sending songs from.
I was woken this morning by the avenue's clamoring drums
and the chitchat of magpies in the courtyard interrupts my spring
    sorrow.
How could I keep up with the human realm,
myself? I am an unmoored boat ten thousand miles away.

---

1   The specific allusion is Ruan Zhao. See note 1 in "Hearing that Censor Li was Back."

代人悼亡

曾睹夭桃想玉姿
帶風楊柳認蛾眉
珠歸龍窟知誰見
鏡在鸞飛話向誰
從此夢悲烟雨夜
不堪吟苦寂寥時
西山日落東山月
恨想無因有了期

---

1   *Zhuangzi*: "A pearl worth a thousand in gold could only have come from under the chin of the Black Dragon who lives at the bottom of the ninefold deeps" 夫千金之珠，必在九重之淵而驪龍頷下 (Watson 2013, 285; Guo and Wang 2012, 1065).

An Elegy on Behalf of Someone

I saw a ripened peach one time. I imagined her poise of jade
and knew her mothwing eyebrows just as willows curve in the wind.
Now the pearl returns to the dragon den[1]—we know, but can
    we see it?
The mirror remains but the simurgh has flown, with no one here to
    speak with.[2]
From now on dreams will be sad. Nights of mist and rain,
unbearable pains and moaning[3] when alone . . .
The sun sets over western mountains, and while the moon is in
    the east
regret and imagination come to an end, without reason.

---

2   The "simurgh" is a bird from Persian mythology whose name sinologists have adopted
to translate *luan*. The *luan* is a bird similar to though slightly lower in status than the
fenghuang (鳳凰, phoenix), and symbolizes elegance, literary cultivation, and marital
harmony, as the *luan* is said to mate for life. Not only is the "simurgh mirror" a mirror
belonging to a refined lady, mythology says that a single *luan* could not bear to see itself
in a mirror, as it would highlight the fact that its mate had died.

3   Her phrase reverses that of "taking pains in composition" of poetry; see note 2 in "Winter
Night, Sent to Wen Tingyun."

和人

茫茫九陌無知己
暮去朝來典繡衣
寶匣鏡昏蟬鬢亂
博山爐暖麝烟微
多情公子春留句
少思文君晝掩扉
莫惜羊車頻列載
柳絲梅綻正芳菲

---

1 Referring to the Tang capital, Chang'an, even though the main city had twelve lateral streets.
2 A hairstyle in which strands from the temples thin as cicada wings are pulled loose from an updo.

Rhyming with Someone

The nine rows[1] stretch out forever, but no one knows me,
leaving at evening and coming back in the morning. I've pawned my
    embroidered robes,
my jewel box mirror is murky, my cicada wing temples[2] are in
    disarray,
and my mountain censer[3] is warm but the musk smoke's gotten thin.
A rounder left some springtime words,
but Wenjun[4] wasn't thinking and shut her gate that day.
Don't spare your carriage[5] for yet another ride:
Threading willows and bursting plums are fragrant, just in time.

3   A container for burning incense, with a conical lid that looked like mountains.
4   Zhuo Wenjun 卓文君 (fl. 2nd century BCE), of the Western Han, eloped with poet and
    statesman Sima Xiangru 司馬相如 (c. 179–117 BCE) as a young widow. Yu is referring to
    herself here.
5   Some understand this to be a cart pulled by rams, but Walls explains that it is a "beau-
    tifully decorated small carriage used within the palace grounds," which Yu uses "as an
    ornate way of saying 'your expensive carriage'" (Walls 1972, 252).

隔漢江寄子安

江南江北愁望
相思相憶空吟
鴛鴦暖臥沙浦
鸂鶒閑飛橘林
烟裏歌聲隱隱
渡頭月色沉沉
含情咫尺千里
況聽家家還砧

Across the Han River—for Li Yi[1]

Sad gazes north and south on the river:
I sing pointless songs of missing you and memories of us.
Mandarin ducks sleep in the warmth of delta sands
and tufted ducks fly through orange groves,
singsong lost in the mist as
the moonlight is dim at the ferry crossing.
At an inch away it feels like a thousand miles,
and still I hear the pounding of laundry[2] from each and every home.

---

1   The Han River cuts through Hubei, where Yu lived from 858 to 862 to be near Li Yi. The
poem features six-character lines, a rare form in medieval Chinese poetics.
2   This places the poem in autumn; see note 2 in "A Boudoir Complaint."

寓言

紅桃處處春色
碧柳家家月明
樓上新妝待夜
閨中獨坐含情
芙蓉葉下魚戲
蠨蝀天邊雀聲
人世悲歡一夢
如何得作雙成

A Parable[1]

Red peaches everywhere, the image of spring
with jade-green willows at every home, and a bright moon.
One awaiting nightfall in fresh makeup upstairs,
another sitting in anticipation alone in the boudoir
but fish play under lotus leaves
and beside a rainbow sky there's sparrow song.
In this world happiness and pain are but a dream,
yet how is it that in gaining one, both arrive?[2]

---

1 This is another poem of six characters per line.

2 "Both Arrive" is also the minor Daoist deity Dong Shuangcheng 董雙成, said to be a handmaiden to the Western Mother Queen 西王母 (generally translated as "Queen Mother of the West," though she is not a Queen Mother, or dowager). The *Zhejiang Chronicles* (*Zhejiang tongzhi* 浙江通志, c. 1550s) explain that "having refined the pill of immortality she attained the way, and flew away on a crane playing *sheng* pipes made of jade" 丹成得道，自吹玉笙，駕鶴飛去. She also appears in the "Rhapsody on Brocade Boots" 錦鞋賦, by Wen Tingyun.

江陵愁望寄子安

楓葉千枝復萬枝
江橋掩映暮帆遲
憶君心似西江水
日夜東流無歇時

Sad Longings at Jiangling—for Li Yi

A thousand branches of sweet-gum leaves, then ten thousand.
The river bridge hides these slow sailboats at dusk.
Remembering you, my heart is like the waters of the west river[1]
flowing east both night and day, with never time for rest.

---

1 The Yangzi River.

寄子安

醉別千巵不浣愁
離腸百結解無由
蕙蘭銷歇歸春圃
楊柳東西絆客舟
聚散已悲雲不定
恩情須學水長流
有花時節知難遇
未肯厭厭醉玉樓

For Li Yi

I left drunk. A thousand goblets couldn't rinse away my sorrow:
departing tied my gut in a hundred knots that couldn't be undone.
Orchids wither and will only return to gardens in spring,[1]
while willows tether travelers' boats both east and west:
with or without you, I grieve for the instability of clouds
despite how in love we must learn from the endless tide.
When flowers are in season I know it's hard to meet,
but don't expect me to sit here sloshed in my jade tower.

1 Yu's childhood name was "Orchid."

送別二首

秦樓幾夜愜心期
不料仙郎有別離
睡覺莫言雲去處
殘燈一盞野蛾飛

水柔逐器知難定
雲出無心肯再歸
惆悵春風楚江暮
鴛鴦一隻失羣飛

---

1 Where Nongyu 弄玉, daughter of Duke Mu of Qin 秦穆公, lived with her husband Xiao Shi 蕭史. It was first called Phoenix 鳳樓 Tower but later became known as Qin Tower. The phrase eventually became a euphemism for a brothel.

Seeing You Off: Two Poems

Amidst nights of satisfaction in Qin Tower[1]
I didn't expect my immortal to go away.
When you wake, don't talk about where the clouds might have gone,
like some moth flittering around a sputtering lamp.

The shape of water conforms to its container:[2] we know it is
    indeterminate.
Clouds drift with no intent.[3] Will they ever come back?
Despondent spring winds over the Chu river this evening,
one mandarin duck strays from its flock.

2   The Legalist classic *Han Feizi* 韓非子 (third century BCE) attributes a quote to Confucius that "In treating the people, the ruler is like the vessel while the populace is like water: if the vessel is rectilinear, the water will be rectilinear; if the vessel is round the water will be round" 為人君者猶盂也，民猶水也，盂方水方，盂圓水圓 (Wang and Zhong 1998, 307). Critics generally read Yu's usage here to mean that women must rely on men to keep them proper.

3   In the famous poem "Returning Home" 歸去來辭 by Tao Qian 陶潛 (a.k.a. Tao Yuan-ming 陶淵明, 365–427) is the couplet "Clouds drift with no intent beyond the peak of the mountain / and birds tire of flying but still know how to return" 雲無心以出岫 鳥倦飛而知還. Yu has tweaked the meaning considerably.

迎李近仁員外

今日喜時聞喜鵲
昨宵燈下拜燈花
焚香出戶迎潘岳
不羨牽牛織女家

A Welcome for Sir Li Jinren[1]

Today in a joyous moment I hear joyous magpies
and under the lamp was visited by lamp blossoms last night.[2]
I light some incense before going to greet Pan Yue.[3]
I do not envy the herd boy and the weaver girl![4]

---

1 No record has been found of this individual. The title *yuanwai* was sometimes an abbreviation of "auxiliary secretary of a ministry" 員外郎, but it was at least as often a title purchased or simply adopted by men who did not otherwise have titles or appointments.
2 The sputtering of flame when the wick burns out, considered an auspicious omen.
3 A poet of the Western Jin; see note 3 in "Rhymes Mourning a New Graduate."
4 Personifications of the stars Altair and Vega, respectively; see note 3 in "Rhyming with My New Neighbor to the West."

左名場自澤州至京使人傳語

閑居作賦幾年愁
王屋山前是舊遊
詩詠東西千嶂亂
馬隨南北一泉流
曾陪雨夜同歡席
別後花時獨上樓
忽喜扣門傳語至
為憐鄰巷小房幽
相如琴罷朱弦斷
雙燕巢分白露秋
莫倦蓬門時一訪
每春忙在曲江頭

Zuo Mingchang Sends a Messenger en Route to the Capital from Zezhou[1]

I've spent my idle life writing poems, but these have been
    sorrowful years.
Our trip to Mount Wangwu[2] was so long ago,
poems singing of a thousand mountain ranges scattered east and
    west, as
our horses traced a north–south line along a single spring.
At that banquet one rainy night we kept each other company,
but after you left when the flowers were in season I've been going
    upstairs alone.
Suddenly now I'm happy when your messenger knocks on the door
of my pitiful home at the dark end of this lane.
Xiangru put his zither down—his red strings snapped
and two swallows broke their nest[3] in the white autumn dew.
Don't mind my rickety gate—come whenever you like,
it's always busy here in spring by Bent River.[4]

---

1   Zuo Mingchang is unidentified. Zezhou is in southwest Shanxi province.
2   A famous site in Daoism, on the Shanxi–Henan border.
3   Yu uses this allusion to Sima Xiangru and Zhuo Wenjun to say that Li Yi has left her; see note 4 in "Rhyming with Someone."
4   Southeast of Chang'an, the place of banquets to honor new graduates of the imperial exam each spring.

和人次韻

喧喧朱紫雜人寰
獨自清吟月色間
何事玉郎搜藻思
忽將瓊韻扣柴關
白花發詠慚稱謝
僻巷深居謬學顏
不用多情欲相見
松蘿高處是前山

1 In the Tang, officials wore red and purple.
2 An immortal of a certain rank in Daoist mythology; also a handsome man, colloquially.

Following Someone Else's Rhyme Words

A cacophony of red and purple[1] at mix in the human realm—
I recite pristine words alone, in the light of the moon.
But why is this man of jade[2] scouring his embellished thoughts
and knocking on my brushwood gate with his gemstone rhymes?
White flowers may inspire my poems, but you embarrass me calling
    me Xie![3]
I live in a back alley, as if I'd followed Yan Hui[4] by mistake.
No need to be so passionate! If you want to meet,
the beard lichen reaches no higher than this mountain before you.

3   Xie Daoyun 謝道韞 (fl. 340–399), favored niece of Eastern Jin prime minister Xie An 謝安 (320–385). The reference here is to her reputation as a great poet, exemplified in the anecdote of her uncle quizzing her and her siblings on how to write a line describing snow. "Sprinkled salt in the sky, that's what it's like" 撒鹽空中差可擬, her brother said; Daoyun replied, "Not unlike willow catkins rising in the wind" 未若柳絮因風起. She was only eight.

4   Yan Hui 顏回 (521–481 BCE), favorite disciple of Confucius. He lived in a humble alley and spent his time in study.

90 HIDING IN CAVERNS FORMED FROM OLD ROOTS

光威哀姊妹三人少孤而始妍乃有是作精粹難儔雖謝
家聯雪何以加之有客自京師來者示予因次其韻

昔聞南國容華少
今日東鄰姊妹三
妝閣相看鸚鵡賦
碧窗應繡鳳凰衫
紅芳滿院參差折
綠醑盈杯次第銜
恐向瑤池曾作女
謫來塵世未為男
文姬有貌終堪比
西子無言我更慚
一曲艷歌琴杳杳
四弦輕撥語喃喃
當臺競鬬青絲髮
對月爭誇白玉簪

1   For the poem to which Yu is responding, see Appendix 1. For the couplet by the Xies,
    see note 3 in "Following Someone Else's Rhyme Words," above.
2   The only extant work by Mi Heng 禰衡 (c. 173–198) of the Eastern Han.

Guang, Wei, and Pou, Sisters Orphaned Young Who Are Growing into Beauties, Wrote a Work of Such Peerless Quintessence that Even the Snow Couplet by the Xie Family Could Add Nothing to It, So I Wrote This Following Its Rhymes After It Was Shown to Me by a Visitor from the Capital[1]

We all heard how rare fine faces were in the south,
but now three sisters have moved in to the east.
They read "Rhapsody of the Parrot"[2] in their boudoir
and embroider phoenix blouses at the emerald window,
and in a fragrant garden pick red blossoms off uneven branches,
sipping from cups they've filled with green wine, one after another.
Maidens at Chalcedony Pool,[3] they were
exiled to the world of dust before they had been turned into men.
Wenji[4] was pretty (but not beyond compare),
and Xi Shi[5] wordless (yes, she shames me more):
is that a strain of distant zither music
or the gentle strumming of four pipa strings, murmuring their words?
They bicker before the mirror over their black silk hair
but boast about hairpins jade white under the moon.

3 The pool, supposed to be in the Kunlun mountains, was associated with the Western
   Mother Queen (for whom, see note 2 in "A Parable").
4 Cai Yan 蔡琰 (c. 178–after 206, or c. 170–215, or died c. 249), one of the few canonical
   women poets of ancient China.
5 The legendary beauty of the fifth century BCE. See note 1 in "At the Temple of Washing Silk."

小有洞中松露滴

大羅天上柳烟含

但能為雨心長在

不怕吹簫事未諧

阿母幾嗔花下語

潘郎曾向夢中參

暫持清句魂猶斷

若睹紅顏死亦甘

悵望佳人何處在

行雲歸北又歸南

---

6   A famous cave, located in Mount Wangwu, said to be where Daoist transcendents reside. It is the first of the ten major cavern heavens.

7   The highest heaven in Daoism.

8   Rain also goes back and forth between the realms of heaven and earth.

Pines in Microcosmos Grotto[6] drip with dew
and Grand Veil Heaven[7] is full of mist-like willow catkins:
as long as their mind of becoming rain remains,[8]
why fear misunderstanding the flute?[9]
Mother[10] scolded them for talking in the flowers
with a Pan Yue,[11] visiting as if in dreams.
But just hold up their pure verse—it would snap such souls in two,
and after a look at their red cheeks, even death might be so sweet.
But now I look off in sorrow. Where have these beauties gone?
The drifting clouds have gone back north, and they have gone
    back south.

9   The reference is to the same story alluded to in note 1 in "Seeing You Off." Xiao Shi (his
    family name means "flute") and his wife Nongyu were so good at playing the flute that
    they could summon phoenixes. One day Nongyu got on the back of a phoenix and Xiao
    Shi mounted a dragon, and they rode off into the heavens.
10 In Daoist contexts, the term refers to Western Mother Queen. It seems especially mean-
    ingful since the sisters were orphans.
11 See note 3 in "Rhymes Mourning a New Graduate."

折楊柳

朝朝送別泣花鈿
折盡春風楊柳烟
願得西山無樹木
免教人作淚懸懸

To Break Willow Branches[1]

Every morning I see you out. I cry into my flower hairclip
at all the willow catkins the spring breeze has broken off.
But I would have all West Mountain bare of trees
so it wouldn't make me shed these streams of tears.

---

1 Because "to stay" (*liu* 留) and "willow" (*liu* 柳) are pronounced similarly, the custom
was to break a willow branch when bidding someone farewell.

逸詩斷句

焚香登玉壇
端簡禮金闕

明月照幽隙
清風開短襟

綺陌春望遠
瑤徽春興多

殷勤不得語
紅淚一雙流

雲情自鬱爭同夢
仙貌長芳又勝花

Fragments

Burning incense, I climb the jade altar,
raise the text, and bow to the Golden Palace.

Moonlight shines through the darkened gap:
a breeze opens the fold of my robe.[1]

Gazing far past springtime's crisscrossed paths,
an agate emblem evokes so much of spring.

Solicitous, yet I say nothing:
a pair of streaming red tears.

Clouds of passion and depression—how can they share a dream?
But the transcendent's manner is always exquisite, beyond even that
of flowers.

---

1 These lines were said to have been written in prison. See Appendix 2.

聯句

光、威、哀，姊妹三人，失其姓

朱樓影直日當午	玉樹陰低月已三	（光）
膩粉暗銷銀鏤合	錯刀閑翦泥金衫	（威）
繡床怕引烏龍吠	錦字愁教青鳥銜	（哀）
百味鍊來憐益母	千花開處鬪宜男	（光）
鴛鴦有伴誰能羨	鸚鵡無言我自慚	（威）
浪喜遊蜂飛撲撲	佯驚孤鵲語喃喃	（哀）
偏憐愛數蟋蟀掌	每憶光抽玳瑁簪	（光）
烟洞幾年悲尚在	星橋一夕帳空含	（威）
窗前時節羞虛擲	世上風流笑苦諳	（哀）
獨結香綃偷餉送	暗垂檀袖學通參	（光）
須知化石心難定	却是爲雲分易甘	（威）
看見風光零落盡	弦聲猶逐望江南	（哀）

Appendix 1: Linked Lines

The Sisters Guang, Wei, and Pou (their surname lost)

Guang: The crimson tower's shadow is straight—the sun is overhead—but the shade of the jade trees has been low for three months.

Wei: A thick powder secretly fuses silver engravings closed while crossed blades snip at mud-stained golden robes.

Pou: On an embroidered bed I fear making the black dragon grunt and in my grief try teaching the blue-green bird to carry brocade words.

Guang: One hundred flavors reduced into a mother's overflowing love, but we fight over a man where a thousand flowers bloom.

Wei: Mandarin ducks have their companions, and everyone envies them, but when parrots are silent, only I feel shame.

Pou: Carefree and happy, bees are all aflutter, while a single magpie murmurs, feigning surprise.

Guang: I've always loved palm turtles and think of them whenever I pull out my tortoiseshell hairpin.

Wei: The pain is still there from years inside a misty cave, while for just one night the bridge of stars is held in the canopy of the sky.

Pou: Before the window this season I'm embarrassed for wasting time. The passions in the world, the suffering, the laughter, I know them all quite well.

Guang: I knot a strand of fragrant silk to make a secret offering alone, sandalwood sleeves hanging in hiding, modeling participation.

Wei: Know the stone of transformation, that a heart is hard to settle, but also that it is easily sweetened once clouds part.

Pou: I see the greatness of the landscape end in desolation, but the sound of strings still follows me, as I gaze to the south of the river.

魚玄機笞斃綠翹致戮，選自《三水小牘》
皇甫枚

西京咸宜觀女道士魚玄機，字幼微，長安里家女也。色既傾國，思乃入神。喜讀書屬文，尤致意於一吟一咏。破瓜之歲，志慕清虛。

咸通初，遂從冠帔于咸宜，而風月賞翫之佳句，往往播於士林。然蕙蘭弱質，不能自持，復為豪俠所調，乃從游處焉。

於是風流之士，爭修飾以求狎，或載酒詣之者，必鳴琴賦詩，間以謔浪，懵學輩自視缺然。其詩有「綺陌春望遠，瑤徽秋興多」。又「殷勤不得語，紅淚一雙流」。又「焚香登玉壇，端簡禮金闕」。又云：

Appendix 2: Yu Xuanji is executed for flogging Lüqiao to death, from *The Little Tablet from Three Waters*

Huangfu Mei

The female Daoist Yu Xuanji, styled Yaowei, of the All Suited Convent of the Western Capital, was a daughter of a family from the streets of Chang'an. Her beauty could have toppled kingdoms, but her thoughts entered the spirit world. She enjoyed reading and literature, and was particularly interested in chanting and recitation. After coming of age, she became intent on contemplating the void.

At the beginning of the Xiantong era she left home and put on Daoist robes at All Suited. Her fine lines about viewing the moon in the charming breeze circulated among literati. But she was fragile and could not restrain herself, and so was easily charmed by heroic men, following them where they might travel.

So the gallants among the scholars would proposition her, trying to outdo each other in how they dressed and bringing drinks when they called on her. She would play the zither and compose poetry, with jokes that might cause some to realize how much they still had to learn. Her poems had lines like:

> Gazing far past springtime's crisscrossed paths,
> an agate emblem evokes so much of spring.

and

> Solicitous, yet I say nothing:
> a pair of streaming red tears

and

> Burning incense, I climb the jade altar,
> raise the text, and bow to the Golden Palace

as well as

「雲情自鬱爭同夢，仙貌長芳又勝花」。此數聯為絕矣。

一女僮曰綠翹，亦特明慧有色。忽一日，機為鄰院所邀，將行，誡翹曰：「無出，若有熟客，但云在某處。」

機為女伴所留，迨暮方歸院，綠翹迎門，曰：「適某客來，知鍊師不在，不舍彎而去矣。」

客乃機素相暱者，意翹與之私。及夜，張燈扃戶，乃命翹入臥內，訊之。翹曰：「自執巾盥數年，實自檢御，不令有似是之過，致忤尊意。且某客至，款扉，翹隔闔報云：『鍊師不在。』客無言，策馬而去。若云情愛，不蓄於胸襟有年矣，幸鍊師無疑。」

機愈怒，裸而笞百數，但言無之。

既委頓，請杯水酹地曰：「鍊師欲求三清長生之道，而未能忘解佩薦枕之歡。反以沈猜，厚誣貞正。翹今必斃於毒手矣！無天則無所訴，若有，誰能抑我彊魂，誓不蠢蠢於冥冥之中，縱爾淫佚。」言訖，絕于地。

機恐，乃坎後庭，瘞之，自謂人無知者。時咸通戊子春正月也。

有問翹者，則曰：「春雨霽，逃矣。」客有宴于機室者，因溲於後庭，當瘞上見青蠅數十集于地，驅去復來；詳視之，如有血痕，且腥。客既出，竊語其僕。僕歸，復語其兄。

APPENDIX 2 103

Clouds of passion and depression—how can they share a dream?
But the transcendent's manner is always exquisite, beyond even that
of flowers.

These lines are exceptional.

She had a girl servant called Lüqiao who was particularly bright and beautiful. One day Xuanji had accepted an invitation to visit her neighbor, and as she left, she instructed Lüqiao, "Don't go anywhere. And if anyone we know shows up, just say that I'm out."

Xuanji was detained by the lady who had invited her, only returning to her own courtyard late that evening. Lüqiao welcomed her at the door and told her: "You had a visitor, but when he learned that my Master Alchemist was out, he left before he could even drop the bridle from his hand."

The visitor was someone Xuanji had known a long time, but it seemed to her that Lüqiao had wanted to be with him. That night, with the lamps lit and doors bolted, Lüqiao was ordered into the bedroom. Questioned, Lüqiao answered, "I have kept myself clean for years, careful to be cautious and controlled, to be sure you would never think I had ever made an error or gone against your wishes. When the visitor arrived he knocked on the door, and I responded from the other side, 'The Master Alchemist is not here.' He said nothing, got back on his horse, and left. If you're talking about love for you, he hasn't had any in his heart for years—fortunately you've never suspected!"

Xuanji grew furious, stripped the girl naked, and flogged her a hundred times. The girl didn't say a word.

When Xuanji took a break, Lüqiao asked her for a cup of water, only to pour it on the ground. "The Master Alchemist has sought the Three Purities Way of Eternal Life," she said, "but you have never forgotten the joys of removing jade pendants and offering your pillows. You drown in suspicion and slander the chaste and upright—I will die today at your poison hands! If there is no heaven, then no one will hear my appeal. But if there is, who can keep my spirit down? I swear I will not sit writhing in the underworld while you indulge your lust!" With these words, she collapsed on the ground.

Xuanji was horrified, and buried her in the backyard, telling herself that no one would find out. This was in the spring of the Wuzi year of Xiantong.

Whenever anyone asked about Lüqiao, Xuanji would only say, "She just disappeared after the spring rains." But when a visitor dining at Xuanji's went to relieve himself in the backyard one time, he found a swarm of flies right above where Lüqiao had been buried, and even when he shooed them away they came right back. Taking a closer look, he noticed traces of blood and a rank smell. As soon as he left, he whispered about it to his servant, who then told his brother.

其兄為府街卒，嘗求金於機，機不顧。卒深銜之。

闻此，遽至觀門覘伺，見偶語者，乃訝不睹綠翹之出入。街卒復呼數卒，攜鍤具，突入玄機院，發之，而綠翹貌如生平。卒遂錄玄機京兆府，吏詰之，辭伏，而朝士多為言者。府乃表列上。至秋，竟戮之。

在獄中亦有詩曰：「易求無價寶，難得有心郎。」「明月照幽隙，清風開短襟。」此其美者也。

APPENDIX 2   105

The brother was a police officer who had once tried to borrow money from Xuanji but had been turned down, and so he had long resented her.

Hearing all this, he rushed to the convent gates to poke around and make inquiries, and everyone he happened to ask was surprised to note that they hadn't seen Lüqiao for so long. The officer ordered a raid on Xuanji's compound. They rushed in with shovels to see what they could dig up—and there was Lüqiao, looking like she did when still alive. The officer wrote up Xuanji and brought her in for questioning at the Jingzhao headquarters, where she threw herself on the mercy of the court. Many literati tried to speak on her behalf, but ultimately the case was submitted. By autumn, she had been executed.

Even in prison, she wrote poems:

Acquiring priceless treasures is easy:
what's hard is finding a man with a heart.

Moonlight shines through the darkened gap:
a breeze opens the fold of my robe.[1]

That was her beauty.

---

1   This conflates lines from "To the Neighbor Girl" and one of the fragments.

選自《北夢瑣言》

孫光憲

唐女道魚玄機，字蕙蘭，甚有才思。咸通中，為李億補闕執箕帚，後愛衰下山，隸咸宜觀為女道士。

有怨李公詩曰：「易求無價寶，難得有心郎。」又云：「蕙蘭銷歇歸春圃，楊柳東西絆客舟。」

自是縱懷，乃娼婦也。竟以殺侍婢為京兆尹溫璋殺之。有集行於世。

Appendix 3: From *Trivialities of North Dream*
Sun Guangxian

In the Tang there was a female Daoist named Yu Xuanji, styled Huilan, who was a talented thinker. During the Xiantong era she filled a need for Li Yi, holding basket and broom for him. Later, when his love dwindled, she came down the mountain and served at the All Suited Convent as a priestess.

She grieved over Li Yi in a poem:

> Acquiring priceless treasures is easy:
> what's hard is finding a man with a heart.

And in another:

> Orchids wither and will only return to gardens in spring,
> while willows tether travelers' boats both east and west.

After this she grew indulgent and became a whore. Later she killed a servant girl, and so was executed by Wen Zhang, magistrate of Jingzhao. Her poetry still circulates.

魚玄機賦

翟永明

一、一條魚和另一條魚的玄機無人知道

　　這是關於被殺和殺人的故事

　　西元八六八年

　　魚玄機　身穿枷衣

　　被送上刑場　躺在血泊中

　　鮮花鉤住了她的人頭

　　很多古代女人身穿枷衣

　　飄滿天空　串起來

　　可以成為白色風箏　她們升不上天

　　魚玄機　身穿道袍　詩文候教

　　十二著文章　十六為人妾

　　二十入道觀　二十五

　　她斃命於黃泉

　　許多守候在螢幕旁的眼睛

　　盯住蕩婦的目錄

　　那些快速移動的指甲

　　剝奪了她們的性

　　她們的名字　落下來

　　成為鍵盤手的即興彈奏

　　根老了　魚群藏匿至它的洞窟

　　魚玄機　想要上天入地

Appendix 4: The Rhapsody of Yu Xuanji

Zhai Yongming

I. The abstruse mystery no one knows between a fish and another fish

This is a story about killing and being killed
868 CE
Yu Xuanji   wears a cangue
is sent to the execution ground   lies in a pool of blood
her severed head on a hook of fresh flowers

So many ancient women wore cangues
strung up   they would fill the sky
like white kites   but never ascending to heaven

Yu Xuanji   wearing Daoist robes   awaits instruction in poetry
composing at twelve   at sixteen a concubine
Daoist convent at twenty   at twenty-five
her life taken   to the Underworld Springs

How many eyes keep watch by the screen
staring at the list of women of ill repute
their swiftly moving fingernails
depriving them of sexuality
their names   fallen
become improvised strokes by keyboard hands

Old roots   schools of fish concealed in their cave
Yu Xuanji   wants to be able to do it all in heaven and on earth

手指如鉤　攪亂了老樹的倒影
一網打盡的　不僅僅是四面八方
圍攏來的眼睛　還有史書的筆墨
道學家們的資料
九月　黃色衣衫飄然階前
她賦詩一首　她的老師看出不祥

歲月固然青蔥但如此無力
花朵有時痛楚卻強烈如焚
春雨放晴　就是她們的死期
「朝士多為言」那也無濟於事
魚玄機著白衣
綠翹穿紅衣
手起刀落　她們的魚鱗
褪下來　成為漫天大雪
螢幕前守候的金屬眼睛
看不見雪花的六面晶體
噴吐墨汁的天空
剝奪了她們的顏色
一條魚和另一條魚
她們之間的玄機
就這樣　永遠無人知道

APPENDIX 4

fingers like hooks   disturbing the reflections of old trees
caught in the web   not only eyes from
all quarters but also   ink traces from history books
Daoist material
yellow robes billowing before the steps   in the ninth month
she composes a poem   her teacher senses an ill omen

The years were as verdant as scallions but just as powerless
flowers are in anguish sometimes but they burn like cinders
when spring rains clear   they're at their time of death
"many literati tried to speak on her behalf"   but to no avail
Yu Xuanji is wearing white
Lüqiao is dressed in red
the hand rises   the knife comes down   their scales
shedding   into a snow-filled sky
metal eyes keeping watch before the screen
don't see the hexagonal snowflake crystals
the ink-spewing sky
deprives them of color
one fish and then another
the abstruse mystery between them
that's the way it is   no one will ever know

二、何必寫怨詩？

這裡躺著魚玄機　她想來想去
決定出家入道　為此
她心中明朗燦爛　又何必寫怨詩？

慵懶地躺在臥室中
拂塵乾枯地跳來跳去　她可以舉起它
乘長風飛到千里之外
寄飛卿、窺宋玉、迎潘岳
訪趙煉師或李郢
對弈李近仁　不再憶李億
又何必寫怨詩？

男人們像走馬燈
他們是畫中人
年輕的丫環　有自己的主意
年輕的女孩　本該如此
她和她　她們都沒有流淚
夜晚本該用來清修
素心燈照不到素心人

魚玄機　她像男人一樣寫作
像男人一樣交遊
無病時，也高臥在床
懶梳妝　樹下奔突的高燒
是毀人的力量　暫時
無人知道　她半夜起來梳頭

APPENDIX 4   113

II. Why write poems of complaint?

Here lies Yu Xuanji   she is thinking
about becoming a priestess   and over this
her heart dazzles   so why write poems of complaint?

Lazily lying in her bedroom
a horsetail whisk drily skipping around   she can lift it
and ride the long wind one thousand miles away
can write to Wen Tingyun, peek at Song Yu, greet Pan Yue
visit Alchemist Zhao or Li Ying
play chess with Li Jinren   forget Li Yi
so why write poems of complaint?

Men are like carousel lanterns
they are the figures in paintings
the young maid   with thoughts of her own
young girls   should all be like this
her and her   not one sheds tears
nights are for self-cultivation
the pure-heart lamp never shines on the pure of heart

Yu Xuanji   she writes like a man
socializes like a man
takes the best bed, even when not sick
doesn't bother with makeup under the tree a sudden fever
a ruinous force   for now
no one knows   in the middle of the night she gets up and combs
    her hair

把詩書讀遍
既然能夠看到年輕男子的笑臉
哪能在乎老年男人的身體？
又何必寫怨詩？

志不求金銀
意不恨王昌
慧不拷銀翹
心如飛花　命犯溫璋
懶得自己動手　一切由它
人生一股煙　升起便是落下
也罷　短命正如長壽
又何必寫怨詩？

三、一支花調寄雁兒落
　　——為古箏所譜、綠翹的鬼魂演奏

魚玄機：
蠟燭、薰香、雙陸
骰子、骨牌、博戲
如果我是一個男子
三百六十棋路　便能見高低

綠翹：
那就讓我們得情於梅花
新桃、紅雲、一派春天
不去買山而隱
偏要倚寺而居

reads through books of poetry
she can see young men's smiles
so why care about old men's bodies?
why write poems of complaint?

Ambition seeks neither gold nor silver
intent does not regret Wang Chang
wisdom will not dissect silver willow leaves
heart like the flight of flowers   fate encroached by Wen Zhang
can't be bothered to raise a hand   but everything depends on it
life is a wisp of smoke   rising only to fall
so be it   a short life's as good as a long one
so why write poems of complaint?

III. A Flower Tune for a Fallen Swallow

Composed for guzheng, *performed by Lüqiao's ghost*

Yu Xuanji:
Candle, incense, double sixes
dominoes, dice, a game of chance
if I were a man
you could see who plays better   in 360 moves on the chessboard

Lüqiao:
So let us find love in plum blossoms
in new peaches, red clouds, a patch of spring
you won't buy a mountain plot for your hermitage
but choose to live by the temple

魚玄機：
銀鉤、兔毫、書冊
題詠、讀詩、酬答
如果我是一個男子
理所當然　風光歸我所有

綠翹：
那就讓我們得氣於煙花
爆竹、一聲裂帛　四下歡呼
你為我搜殘詩
我為你譜新曲

合：
有心窺宋玉
無意上旌表
所以犯天條
那就邁開淩波步幅
不再逃也不去逃

四、魚玄機的墓誌銘
這裡躺著詩人魚玄機
她生卒皆不逢時
早生早死八百年
寫詩　作畫　多情
她沒有贏得風流薄倖名
卻吃了冤枉官司
別人的墓前長滿松柏
她的墳上　至今開紅花

Yu Xuanji:
Silver hooks, rabbit hair brushes, books
chanting inscriptions, reciting poems, replying in verse
if I were a man
as a matter of course   the wind and light would all be mine

Lüqiao:
So let us find our breath in gunpowder
in fire crackers, a silk-rending sound   with cheers in four directions
for me you search for scraps of poetry
for you I compose new melodies

Both:
Intentionally peeking at Song Yu
inadvertently conferring an honor
thus violating heaven's commandments
so then we will stride in ripple steps
no more fleeing or trying to flee

IV. Yu Xuanji's epitaph

Here lies Yu Xuanji, the poet
her birth and death were not auspicious
she was born too early and died too early by eight hundred years
writing poems   painting   overinvested in passions
she never gained a reputation as a flirt
just suffered unjust judgments
before others' graves are pine and cypress
but on her tomb   red flowers even still

美女身份遮住了她的才華蓋世
望著那些高高在上的聖賢名師
她永不服氣

五、關於魚玄機之死的分析報告

「這裡躺著魚玄機」當我
在電腦上敲出這樣的文字
我並不知道
她生於何地　葬於何處？

作為一個犯罪嫌疑人　她甚至
沒有律師　不能翻供
作為一個蕩婦　她只能引頸受戮
以正朝綱　視聽　民憤等等

這裡躺著魚玄機　她在地下
大哭或者大罵　大悲或者大笑
我們只能猜測　就象皇甫枚——
一個讓她出名的傢伙
猜測了她和綠翹的對話

當我埋首於一大堆卷宗裡
想像西元八六八年　離我們多遠
萬水千山　還隔著一個又一個偉大的朝代

多麼年輕呵
她賦得江邊柳　卻賦不得男人心
比起那些躺在女子祠堂裡的婦女
她的心一片桃紅

APPENDIX 4

her beauty hid her peerless talent
looking at those lofty sages and renowned masters
she never gave in

V. Analysis on the death of Yu Xuanji

When I typed "Here lies Yu Xuanji"
on my computer
I didn't know
where she had died   where she was buried

A suspected criminal   she never
even had a lawyer   couldn't issue a retraction
A fallen woman   she could only stick out her neck
to uphold order   in the face of public outrage and so on

Here lies Yu Xuanji   she is underground
crying or cursing   grieving or laughing
we can only guess   like Huangfu Mei
just some guy who made her famous
guessing at what she and Lüqiao said

And I bury myself in stacks of documents
imagining 868 CE   how far from us
one thousand mountains ten thousand waters   separated by one
    great dynasty after another

Oh so young
she was granted the willows on the river   but was never granted the
    heart of a man
compared to everyone laid to rest in the Women's Ancestral Halls

這裡躺著魚玄機　她生性傲慢
活該她倒楣　想想別的那些女詩人
她們為自己留下足夠的分析資料
她們才不會理睬什麼皇甫枚

那些風流　那些多情的顏色
把她的道袍變成了萬花筒
多好呵
如果西元八六八　變成了西元二〇〇五
她也許會從現在直活到八十五
有正當的職業　兒女不缺
她的女性意識　雖備受質疑
但不會讓她吃官司　挨杖斃

這裡躺著魚玄機　她在地下
也怨恨著：在唐代
為什麼沒有高科技？
這些猜測和想像
都不能變為呈堂供證
只是一個業餘考據者的分析
在秋天　她必須赴死

這裡躺著魚玄機　想起這些
在地下　她也永不服氣

2005.9.10 於義大利 Civitella 藝術中心

APPENDIX 4

her heart is peach blossom red
Here lies Yu Xuanji   born proud
if she was unlucky, she deserved it   think of all the other women
    poets
They left enough material for analysis
they would never pay heed to Huangfu Mei

Those charismas those sentimental colors
made a kaleidoscope of her Daoist robes
how lovely
if only 868 CE   could be 2005
she could have lived to 85
with a proper profession   and any number of children
her feminist consciousness   though interrogated
would not have led to indictments   to death by the rod

Here lies Yu Xuanji   she is underground
and full of regret: why was nothing
high tech in the Tang?
these speculations and imaginations
are not admissible as evidence
they are just the analyses of an amateur examiner
in autumn   she had to die

Here lies Yu Xuanji   thinking back on all this
underground   she will never give in

September 10, 2005, Civitella Ranieri Foundation, Italy

Bibliography

Editions

Chen Wenhua 陳文華, ed. 1984. *Tang nüshiren ji sanzhong* 唐女詩人集三種 *[Three Women Poets of the Tang]*. Shanghai guji chubanshe.

Translations

Carpenter, Jennifer, trans. 1999. "Yu Xuanji." In *Women Writers of Traditional China: An Anthology of Poetry and Criticism*, edited by Kang-i Sun Chang, Haun Saussy, and Charles Yim-tze Kwong, 66–75. Stanford University Press.

Chow, Bonnie, and Thomas Cleary, trans. 2003. *Autumn Willows: Poetry by Women of China's Golden Age*. Story Line Press.

Farman, Michael, ed. Grace S. Fong, Emily Goedde, Jeanne Larsen, Geoffrey Waters, and Michael Farman, trans. 2013. *Jade Mirror: Women Poets of China*. White Pine Press.

Harris, R. Earle [Hei Fengcong 黑瘋聰], trans. 2015. "Poems of Yu Xuanji." Tang Dynasty Poetry. 2015. https://tangshi.tuxfamily.org/yuxuanji/.

Idema, Wilt L., and Beata Grant. 2004. *The Red Brush: Writing Women of Imperial China*. Harvard University Asia Center.

Karashima Takeshi 辛島驍, trans. 1964. *Gyo Genki-Setsu Tō* 魚玄機, 薛濤 *[Yu Xuanji, Xue Tao]*. Shūeisha.

Kelen, Kit, Hilda Tam 譚曉汶, and Chris Song 宋子江, trans. 2010. *Yu Xuanji: Hard to Find a Loving Man*. Association of Stories in Macao.

Larsen, Jeanne, trans. 2015. *Willow, Wine, Mirror, Moon: Women's Poems from Tang China*. BOA Editions, Ltd.

Ng, Leonard, trans. 2016. "The Complete Poems of Yu Xuanji." Leonard Ng. 2016. https://www.leonard-ng.com/complete-poems-of-yu-xuanji/.

Nie, Rebecca, and Peter Levitt, trans. 2022. *Yin Mountain: The Immortal Poetry of Three Daoist Women*. Shambhala Publications.

Wimsatt, Genevieve, trans. 1936. *Selling Wilted Peonies: Biography and Songs of Yü Hsuan-Chi, T'ang Poetess*. Columbia University Press.

Young, David, and Jiann I. Lin, trans. 1998. *The Clouds Float North: The Complete Poems of Yu Xuanji*. Wesleyan University Press.

Secondary Scholarship

Jia, Jinhua. 2018. *Gender, Power, and Talent: The Journey of Daoist Priestesses in Tang China*. Columbia University Press.

BIBLIOGRAPHY

Jinling. 2018. "On Studying the Mis-Translation of the Poems of Yu Xuanji through the Comparison of Original Texts and Translation Version." *International Journal on Studies in English Language and Literature* 6 (12): 24–30.

Liu, Yang. 2011. "Imagery of Female Daoists in Tang and Song Poetry." Ph.D. dissertation, University of British Columbia.

Walls, Jan Wilson. 1972. "The Poetry of Yü Hsuan-Chi: A Translation, Annotation, Commentary and Critique." Ph.D. dissertation, Indiana University.

Works Cited

Benn, Charles D. 2004. *China's Golden Age: Everyday Life in the Tang Dynasty.* Oxford University Press.

Bossler, Beverly. 2012. "Vocabularies of Pleasure: Categorizing Female Entertainers in the Late Tang Dynasty." *Harvard Journal of Asiatic Studies* 72 (1): 71–99.

Cahill, Suzanne. 2002. "Material Culture and the Dao: Textiles, Boats, and Zithers in the Poetry of Yu Xuanji (844–868)." In *Daoist Identity: History, Lineage, and Ritual,* edited by Livia Kohn and Harold D. Roth, 102–126. University of Hawai'i Press.

Cain, Abigail. 2017. "What Was the First Abstract Painting?" *Artsy,* March 31, 2017. https://www.artsy.net/article/artsy-editorial-first-abstract-artwork.

Chan, Timothy Wai Keung. 2008. "A Tale of Two Worlds: The Late Tang Poetic Presentation of the Romance of the Peach Blossom Font." *T'oung Pao* 94 (4/5): 209–245.

Chang, Kang-i Sun. 1980. *The Evolution of Chinese Tz'u Poetry: From Late T'ang to Northern Sung.* Princeton University Press.

Chang, Kang-i Sun, Haun Saussy, and Charles Yim-tze Kwong, eds. 1999. *Women Writers of Traditional China: An Anthology of Poetry and Criticism.* Stanford University Press.

Cheng Yi 程頤. Wing-tsit Chan, trans. 2014. "Biographies of My Parents." In *Readings in Later Chinese Philosophy: Han Dynasty to the 20th Century,* edited by Justin Tiwald and Bryan W. Van Norden, 290–92. Hackett Publishing.

Da, Nan Z. 2015. "On the Decipherment of Modern China and Spurned Lovers: Zhai Yongming's *Most Tactful Phrases.*" *Signs* 40 (3): 667–693.

Denecke, Wiebke, and Lucas Klein. 2023. "Launching the Hsu-Tang Library of Classical Chinese Literature on the 250th Anniversary of the Complete Library of the Four Treasuries." *Journal of Asian Studies* 82 (2): 206–217.

Ebrey, Patricia Buckley. 1993. *The Inner Quarters: Marriage and the Lives of Chinese Women in the Sung Period.* University of California Press.

Egan, Ronald. 2013. *The Burden of Female Talent: The Poet Li Qingzhao and Her History in China.* Harvard University Asia Center.

Fenollosa, Ernest, and Ezra Pound. 2008. *The Chinese Written Character as a Medium for Poetry: A Critical Edition,* edited by Haun Saussy, Jonathan Stalling, and Lucas Klein. Fordham University Press.

Fong, Grace S. 2008. *Herself an Author: Gender, Agency, and Writing in Late Imperial China*. University of Hawai'i Press.

Fong, Grace S. 2022. "Feminist Theories and Women Writers of Late Imperial China: Impact and Critique." *Journal of Chinese Literature and Culture* 9 (1): 105–130.

Friedman, Susan Stanford. 1996. "'Beyond' Gynocriticism and Gynesis: The Geographics of Identity and the Future of Feminist Criticism." *Tulsa Studies in Women's Literature* 15, no. 1: 13–40.

Fu Xuancong 傅璇琮, ed. 1999. *Tangren xuan Tangshi xinbian* 唐人選唐詩 新編 *[A New Edition of Tang Poetry as Selected in the Tang]*. Wenshizhe chubanshe.

Guo Qingfan 郭慶藩 and Wang Xiaoyu 王孝魚, eds. 2012. *Zhuangzi jishi* 莊子集 釋 *[The Complete Zhuangzi with Exegesis]*. Zhonghua shuju.

Hinsch, Bret. 2019. *Women in Tang China*. Rowman & Littlefield.

Hurvitz, Leon, trans. 2009. *Scripture of the Lotus Blossom of the Fine Dharma*. Columbia University Press.

Klein, Lucas. 2016. "Tribunals of Erudition and Taste: Or, Why Translations of Premodern Chinese Poetry Are Having a Moment Right Now." *Los Angeles Review of Books*. July 14, 2016. https://lareviewofbooks.org/article/tribunals-of-erudition-and-taste-or-why-translations-of-premodern-chinese-poetry-are-having-a-moment-right-now.

Klein, Lucas. 2018. "Strong and Weak Interpretations in Translating Chinese Poetry." *Journal of Modern Literature in Chinese* 14.2-15.1: 7–43.

Klein, Lucas. 2019. "Mediation Is Our Authenticity: *Dagong* Poetry and the *Shijing* in Translation." In *Chinese Poetry and Translation: Rights and Wrongs*, edited by Maghiel van Crevel and Lucas Klein, 201–222. Amsterdam University Press.

Knechtges, David R., trans. 1996. "Rhapsody on the Gaotang Shrine." In *Wen Xuan, or Selections of Refined Literature*, 3:325–339. Princeton University Press.

Ko, Dorothy. 1994. *Teachers of the Inner Chambers: Women and Culture in Seventeenth-Century China*. Stanford University Press.

Kroll, Paul W. 1988. Review of *Brocade River Poems: Selected Works of the Tang Dynasty Courtesan Xue Tao*, by Jeanne Larsen. *Journal of the American Oriental Society* 108 (4): 621–626.

Kroll, Paul W. 2018. "Translation, or Sinology: Problems of Aims and Results." *Journal of the American Oriental Society* 138 (3): 559–566.

Larsen, Jeanne, trans. 1987. *Brocade River Poems: Selected Works of the Tang Dynasty Courtesan Xue Tao*. Princeton University Press.

Li, Xiaorong. 2013. *Women's Poetry of Late Imperial China: Transforming the Inner Chambers*. University of Washington Press.

Liu, James J. Y. 1982. "The Critic as Translator." In *The Interlingual Critic: Interpreting Chinese Poetry*, 37–49. Indiana University Press.

BIBLIOGRAPHY

Liu, Lydia H. 1993. "Invention and Intervention: The Female Tradition in Modern Chinese Literature." In *Gender Politics in Modern China: Writing and Feminism*, edited by Tani E. Barlow, 33–57. Duke University Press.

Lowell, Amy. 1921. "Preface." In *Fir-Flower Tablets: Poems Translated from the Chinese*, by Florence Ayscough and Amy Lowell, v–x. Houghton Mifflin.

Lowry, Glenn D. 2012. "Foreword." In *Inventing Abstraction 1910–1925: How a Radical Idea Changed Modern Art*, edited by Leah Dickerman, 7. Museum of Modern Art.

Mann, Susan. 1997. *Precious Records: Women in China's Long Eighteenth Century*. Stanford University Press.

Mou, Huaichuan. 2004. *Rediscovering Wen Tingyun: A Historical Key to a Poetic Labyrinth*. State University of New York Press.

Olson, Charles. 1967. "Projective Verse." In *Selected Writings of Charles Olson*, edited by Robert Creeley, 15–26. New Directions.

Owen, Stephen. 2006. *The Late Tang: Chinese Poetry of the Mid-Ninth Century (827–860)*. Harvard University Asia Center.

Owen, Stephen. 2019. *Just a Song: Chinese Lyrics from the Eleventh and Early Twelfth Centuries*. Harvard University Asia Center.

Pound, Ezra. 2003. *Ezra Pound: Poems and Translations*, edited by Richard Sieburth. Library of America.

Rawski, Evelyn Sakakida. 1979. *Education and Popular Literacy in Ch'ing China*. University of Michigan Press.

Rexroth, Kenneth, and Ling Chung, trans. 1972. *The Orchid Boat: Women Poets of China*. McGraw-Hill.

Rich, Adrienne. 1972. "When We Dead Awaken: Writing as Re-Vision." *College English* 34 (1): 18–30.

Robertson, Maureen. 1992. "Voicing the Feminine: Constructions of the Gendered Subject in Lyric Poetry by Women of Medieval and Late Imperial China." *Late Imperial China* 13 (1): 63–110.

Rouzer, Paul F. 1993. *Writing Another's Dream: The Poetry of Wen Tingyun*. Stanford University Press.

Rouzer, Paul F. 2001. *Articulated Ladies: Gender and the Male Community in Early Chinese Texts*. Harvard University Asia Center.

Saussy, Haun. 2001. *Great Walls of Discourse and Other Adventures in Cultural China*. Harvard University Asia Center.

Schafer, Edward H. 1973. *The Divine Woman: Dragon Ladies and Rain Maidens in T'ang Literature*. University of California Press.

Shields, Anna M. 2006. *Crafting a Collection: The Cultural Contexts and Poetic Practice of the* Huajian Ji. Harvard University Asia Center.

Voss, Julia. Anne Posten, trans. 2022. *Hilma Af Klint: A Biography*. University of Chicago Press.

Wang Xianshen 王先慎 and Zhong Zhe 鍾哲, eds. 1998. *Han Feizi jijie* 韓非子集解 *[The Collected and Explicated Han Feizi]*. Zhonghua shuju.

Watson, Burton, trans. 2013. *The Complete Works of Zhuangzi*. Columbia University Press.

Weinberger, Eliot. 2022. *Brice Marden: These Paintings Are of Themselves*. Gagosian/Rizzoli.

Widmer, Ellen. 1989. "The Epistolary World of Female Talent in Seventeenth-Century China." *Late Imperial China* 10 (2): 1–43.

Wixted, John Timothy. 1994. "The Poetry of Li Ch'ing-Chao: A Woman Author and Women's Authorship." In *Voices of the Song Lyric in China*, edited by Pauline Yu, 145–168. University of California Press.

Wu, Fusheng. 1998. *The Poetics of Decadence: Chinese Poetry of the Southern Dynasties and Late Tang Periods*. State University of New York Press.

Xiao Tong 蕭統. 1994. *Wenxuan* 文選 *[Selections of Refined Literature]*. Shanghai guji chubanshe.

Yang, Binbin. 2016. *Heroines of the Qing: Exemplary Women Tell Their Stories*. University of Washington Press.

Yang, Haihong. 2017. *Women's Poetry and Poetics in Late Imperial China: A Dialogic Engagement*. Lexington Books.

Yao Ping 姚平. 2004. *Tangdai funü de shengming licheng* 唐代婦女的生命歷程 *[Life Journeys of Tang Women]*. Shanghai guji chubanshe.

Yip, Wai-lim, ed. 1997. *Chinese Poetry: An Anthology of Major Modes and Genres*. Duke University Press.

Zhai Yongming 翟永明. 2013. "Yu Xuanji fu" 魚玄機賦 [The Rhapsody of Yu Xuanji]. In *Denggao: Zhai Yongming shixuan* 登高: 翟永明詩選 *[Climbing High: The Selected Poems of Zhai Yongming]*, 271–279. Xiuwei chubanshe.